Good Morning

When Power is Not present.
Pain will try to take You Out ╬

Maury Danielle

Gain Through Pain!
By Maury Danielle

Good Morning Nude

Cover design: Sarah Crichlow
SarahStella Creative Studio

Synopsis Editor: Justine Harkness

Editing: Cynthia Valentine
Destiny Publishings LLC

In loving memory of
Carolyn Sue Little Coursey Williams

Appreciation

Where would I be if it had not been for my creator— the precious gift of the Holy Spirit (Guide, Truth, Wisdom, Conviction, Revelation)? So, I would truly be out of order if I didn't first give all praise, glory and honor to my heavenly father. There is a worship song written by Chris Tomlin entitled, "Good, Good Father." It has become the foundation of my relationship with God.

I have had to unlearn the worlds definition of, "love." Opening myself up to experience the true authentic and intimate LOVE of my heavenly father, feels so overwhelming at times. However, there is no greater love than His.

Through life's journey, I am accepting that everything changes. Nothing stays the same. The beauty and power of transformation—what better way to be transformed than through renewing your mind in Christ daily.

I'm thankful for my wonderful spiritual friends. Your divine wisdom, discernment and prayers have been priceless. Without those things, the road that I have traveled at times, would have been intolerable.

To my family. Thank you for always loving me, even when you didn't understand me. Thank you for supporting and being patient with me. From 2014 through 2018, I went through THE hardest times in my life. But then again, the last nine years in total have been filled with challenge after challenge. I have faced many giants, but there is nothing like facing a village or tribe of giants all at once, back to back to back to back. Where would I be if I did not have my earthly support system?

Thank you, Mom, Denise Williams-White, for the precious gift and power of a "praying mother." You have destroyed many generational barriers. Your sacrifice of love through prayer and faith can never be repaid. The greatest gift that you could have ever given to me and your grandchildren is the power of prayer!

I must give thanks to my amazing children, my resilient and spiritually articulate daughter, Amaris Makayla and my energetic and wise son, Amias Elyon. You keep me selflessly going and striving for excellence every day! In my darkest moments, if there were no you, then there would not have been me.

Thank you, Aunty Carol Kay aka "sister and friend." We have walked many valleys and seen many mountaintops together. Thanks for your love, support and sacrifice to both me and my children. Thank you for igniting the flame. Your actions helped me to do the work required for growth and healing.

Thank you, Mari Wingate. It still amazes me that through a simple wooden table set, God chose to connect us in such a divinely appointed way! You are my "sister-friend." You *have a heart of pure Gold for Christ and mankind. You are always setting Godly examples for the Kingdom of God. You are a spiritual mentor and leader to so many. Thank you for the labored time and prayers dedicated to our friendship and to our families.*

Thank you, Dr. Keschia Matthews, for 100-plus ways and more! You are one of my baddest and most glamorous friends. Your anointing blows the roof off church buildings and sets fire alarms off with your inferno prayers. You speak with such spiritual-wisdom, poise and grace. I am elated to see the blessings and favor upon your life. Thank you, Pal!

To all the great spiritual leaders and pioneers that I have had the privilege and honor to sit under. Words cannot express my heart felt love and gratitude for your spiritual covering, by way of your ministry and teachings. Thank you for your spiritual intelligence and wisdom. May Yahweh be praised for your sacrifice and obedience to many families. You have guided and taught men and women for decades. Thank you for your prayers, love and support!! Pastor Deboroux Hubbard - Peoria, IL, Pastor Terrance H. Johnson – Houston, TX, Pastors Greg & Linda Crawford – Missouri City, TX, Pastor Edson Weithers-Houston Texas, Pastor Bayless Conley – Los Alamitos, CA, Pastors Toure & Sarah (Jakes) Roberts –Los Angeles, CA.

To "A Mother's Prayer" and "Sisters That Pray" prayer warriors. Women like you stand in the gap for the masses. God continues to bring heaven to earth and act on behalf of your prayers. Don't ever stop being an intercessor. The power of your prayers changes the atmosphere. You, indeed, have been "called" for the Kingdom of God.

Prayer for the reader

Heavenly Father, I come to you now, in the Name of our Lord and Savior, Christ Jesus.

Lord, life seems so unjust, so unfair and so heavy most times. The pain of rejection is almost more than some can bare. Some relationships and lives have ended in strife, anger, rejection, resentment, and bitterness. Father, help us to let go of all bitterness, resentment, grief, depression, and pain, that may be hindering us from our progression and growth. Those infirmities that may be holding us captive in bondage and despair; paralyzing our movement mentally, physically, emotionally, spiritually and even financially.

You are the one who can heal broken-hearts. We receive your anointing that breaks and destroys every yoke of bondage. We receive emotional healing by faith according to your Word, Isaiah 53:5, "...and with His stripes we are healed." We thank you for giving us the grace to stand firm until this process is complete. We acknowledge, and we thank you for our wise counselor, the Holy Spirit! We ask that you continue to send your ministering and protecting angels around us. Help those who are currently battling grief and depression from suffering loss, trauma or pain. Help those that are being abused mentally, sexually, physically, emotionally, and psychologically.

Today, we make the choice to forgive those who have wronged us. Then, Oh Lord, we pray for the abuser(s) who inadvertently picks up this book and reads it. May they find penitence, forgiveness and help to stop and change. We ask You Heavenly Father and Precious Holy Spirit, to speak to each reader individually through these pages. Minister, heal and set free as only you, oh powerful God can do. Let your anointing fall fresh each time this book is opened and each time these pages are turned.

*I believe my life and my testimony is not in vain. I declare for each reader **Romans 8:28 "And we know that in all things God works for the good of those who love him, who have been called according to his purpose."** We pray in your name, Amen.*

Attention- DISCLAIMER

The author of this book does not give medical advice. The content of this book is not intended to replace medical advice or treatment for depression or any mental illness. The intent of this material is to provide supplemental information. It is the author's desire to aid in emotional and spiritual growth. This is done by the author sharing her personal journey and testimony. It includes healing and overcoming grief, depression, and domestic violence. Again, this book should not be interpreted as medical or therapeutic advice. Please seek professional help when distressed.

If you are contemplating suicide, call 1-800-273-TALK and speak with someone at the National Suicide Prevention Lifeline. There are a lot of good services available. If you are feeling threatened or in danger, please dial 911. The National Domestic Violence Hotline 1-800-799-SAFE. Please reach out to an agency that can connect you with the services that you need.

THANK YOU

Preface

Dear Maury,

It's time to unleash the truth behind your hurt. It's time to apologize for the wrong that I have caused you and to stop focusing on the wrong or pain that others have caused you.

Let me start by saying that I'm truly sorry. I'm truly sorry that from a small child you never understood your value. I'm sorry that those that were meant to protect you, abused their power and hurt you. I'm sorry that I didn't always know how to protect you. I'm sorry that your dad rejected you and your uncle violated you. Through the years many men have been allowed to devalue you. It has taken me almost four decades to realize the hurt and damage that I have caused you. I did this by suppressing memories and keeping silent about things that should have been told. I'm sorry that I have been so busy protecting others that I forgot to protect the most important person, YOU! I'm sorry that I made you look for love and desire to be loved by others. The greatest and most rewarding love should have come from within. I am sorry I never knew how to love you. Instead of addressing and loving you through the pain, it was easier not to love you at all. Being afraid of reaching for God's love and knowing that His love is the beginning of real love, is probably what hurts the most. Disappointments, rejections, hurts, and pain happens to people every day. Without knowing who you are and how to stand, makes you prey. It subjects you to fall for things that were never intended for you.

I spent the majority of your life criticizing you and judging you. I condemned you when you did something wrong or displeasing. In that condemnation, I allowed you to continue down a path of self-destruction. I never stopped to really think, feel, and guide you. The truth is, God's love is unconditional and non-condemning. The biggest mistake of all, is that instead of truly nurturing our relationship with God from the inside out, I allowed you to mask your hurt. That caused a superficial exterior and a false hope interior showing a relationship with God from the outside in. I have allowed you to play small. I knew that you deserved big, but the big things meant patience, stretching, and growing. Great things sometimes take time—and that's ok.

I often told you that you weren't pretty enough. There were times I said you were not thick enough and then at a times small enough, or good enough. I'm sorry that I didn't realize that you were not supposed to look like everyone else. Your creator hand designed you as a special and rare gift. Over the years you have grown to be strong and rise above to reach new heights and new levels. It wasn't grounded so; those things didn't last. When you tried to rise and be strong, I would put all kinds of doubt and fear in your mind instead of supporting you with love. This lack of support and love for the authentic pushed you to attach to the wrong people, places, and things. Subconsciously, I even made you believe that the opinions of others were most important. You've always thrived off your own independence. I made you feel uncomfortable by directing your attention to other's insecurities. This made you own their issues. Therefore, you would shy away in order not to bring too much attention to yourself. I made you believe that if someone hurt you it was entirely your fault. I made you believe that your worth was based on other people's opinions and actions.

I am telling you now, that I was wrong. I was wrong to make you believe that anyone who didn't see you for who you are mattered. You felt broken when someone you loved hurt or betrayed you. You believed your worth depended on the love you received from the world. I see now that the thoughts I formed in you gave you issues of trust. The need to be loved even in unhealthy ways came from experiences that were not your fault. I have learned from these circumstances. They no longer need to define who you are. They no longer need to reflect negatively onto you.

The truth is, you are an amazing, loving soul. All the things you view, as imperfections are what make you the beautiful person that you truly are. The ones who choose to hurt instead of love, are battling their own self-worth issues. I am telling you now to let them go! I realize now the importance of telling you to let go of whatever no longer serves you.

From this day forward, I promise to make choices each day to be more supportive, more encouraging, and more loving to you than the days before. As we have gone through life's cycles together, I am so happy that we have reached this part of our journey. Today, we are full of color and full of life. TODAY we gained our wings. Today we became a Butterfly!

Fly, Forty & Free. A Metamorphosis.......

Sincerely,
Me (Maury Danielle)

Table of Contents

Part 1: Drafted

Chapter One: Warning!!!! Oblique Premonition 19
Chapter Two: Family Ties Generationally Picked 27
Chapter Three: Controlled Conversations
(Peek-A-Boo Private) 37

Part 2: Uncovered Wounds

Chapter Four: Into Darkness The Abyss of Depression .. 47
Chapter Five: Barring Disappointment 63
Chapter Six: Traumas, Triggers and Anger 71

Part 3: Call to Duty

Chapter Seven: UNMUTED 85
Chapter Eight: Good Mourning Nude (Out of the Fog) .. 97
Chapter Nine: From Pit to Power - Olympus Mandate. 109

Part 4: Surviving to Thriving

Postface: Butterfly Free 121
Power Source: Power Scriptures & Names of God…....129
Prayer: A Survivors Prayer:…………………….131

Index
Directory of Help: Resources & Helpful Links
Knowledge: Suggested Readings

Part 1

DRAFTED

Jeremiah 1:5

"I knew you before I formed you in your mother's womb. Before you were born I set you apart and appointed you as my prophet to the nations."

Chapter One

Warning!!!!
Oblique Premonition

Hebrews 3:7-11

Therefore, just as the Holy Spirit says, "TODAY IF YOU HEAR HIS VOICE, DO NOT HARDEN YOUR HEARTS AS WHEN THEY PROVOKED ME, AS IN THE DAY OF TRIAL IN THE WILDERNESS, WHERE YOUR FATHERS TRIED Me BY TESTING Me, AND SAW MY WORKS FOR FORTY YEARS."

October 2009 Dream
"Life Turned Upside Down"

A day after a close friend's mother died, I stayed overnight at her house. I wanted to support her during what would be one of the most difficult times in her life. As I slept that night in her bed, I had a dream that my friend was trapped in her home and refused to leave it. There was a hole in her ceiling. White doves started flying through it. There were nine windowpanes on it. As the birds landed, they began to hang upside down on the windowpanes like bats. There were nine birds in each windowpane, three (3) rows down, three (3) rows across.

A guy friend of mine was also in the dream. Both of us were trying to get my friend to leave her house. We were attempting to save her, but she refused to leave. Eventually, we were able to get her out. When I woke up from that dream, back in 2009, I could hear the Holy Spirit whisper "Life turned upside down!" Little did I know, that dream held a lot of validity and truth for occurrences that would befall me in the coming years.

I leaned on my own ideology as opposed to seeking God to reveal what the dream truly meant. My thoughts were, "this was about my friend." She had just lost her mother. The dream occurred while I was in her home, bed, and in her environment. Therefore, I did not see the need to pray for the interpretation. I later realized how spiritually ignorant and wrong that I was.

My gift as it related to interpreting dreams had not fully matured. I shared this dream with her, even though I wasn't sure of what it meant. Perhaps, she could make sense of it. About a year later, I found myself having flashbacks about the dream. That caused me to question the validity of my mis-interpretation. I tarried in prayer. My plea to God was for Him to reveal what this dream meant.

I literally started to live the words "Life Turned Upside Down." I had to walk it out to get to where I am today. That dream was the spirit of God warning and preparing me of things to come. My last name was predestined to change to "Mourning." The evolving revelation about this dream is what birthed, "Good Mourning Nude." My friend was mourning the loss of her mother. The mourning doves in that dream symbolized "mourning." My last name and life would eventually be flipped upside down. I had a period of significant loss that would lead to severe depression. I experienced healing, rebirth, hope, peace, purpose, and destiny.

Over the years I have learned the value of interpreting dreams by writing the dream down, paying attention to symbols and colors, people and locations, emotions and responses. I have learned that as much as God speaks in the natural, He also speaks through dreams.

I believed my male friend's role in the dream was symbolic because he is a real-life licensed counselor. Together he and my girlfriend that were in the dream symbolized "Godly Counsel."

I would need wise and Godly counsel to help me navigate in the years to come.

I later discovered that the biblical number "nine" that was in my dream was symbolic to wholeness and becoming. The number nine represents three divine manifestations through three plans. Biblically, the number nine has a lot of spiritual insight and significance. Nine signifies recompense, reconciliation, and redemption. Interpretation: The Biblical meaning of the number nine is "finality" or "the fullness of God. The finality of God comes with a connotation of justice and judgment. Jesus died on the cross on the 9th hour of the day. When he died, it was finished! After the sacrifice was finalized on the 9th hour, it was followed by redemption, reconciliation, and recompense. This is given to all who would receive HIM through his sacrifice. Preceding his death, Jesus is noted to have appeared a total of nine times. He was seen by his apostles and disciplines after his resurrection. The New Testament notes that there are nine spiritual gifts of God.

Correspondingly, peace, patience, kindness, goodness, truthfulness, gentleness, and self-control are disciplines that should be practiced in everyday life. In natural birth, the number nine stands for a complete cycle of growth. For me, those nine years of my life being turned upside down all worked together for my good. It certainly did not feel like that a good amount of the time because I suffered deep agony and pain. I was stripped nude figuratively by my circumstances before I even began to see what was transpiring. A total transformation was taking place within me. It would happen over a course of nine antagonizing years. I was at a place of vulnerability when I came to grips. However, it was necessary for me to reach a place of recompense, reconciliation, and redemption. I have certainly come to realize and respect that the biblical number "nine" represents patience. Nine, is also a symbol of creation. It denotes life is full of developments, changes, and rhythm.

The journey of my pain and vulnerability lead me to discover a deeper revelation that had to be addressed. There was a genetic pattern and despondency that was tied to the lineage of my family. What I walked through and would overcome would set my children free. They would not have to walk the same path as myself and generations past. God called me to not only break generational patterns and trauma, but he called me to destroy it!

The spiritual substance of this dream and its symbolism was laborious to digest and to interpret. Those years of my life were literally "flipped upside down." There have been times in my life when a vision flashed before me. I could interpret it's meaning right away. As far as this dream was concerned, I had to pray. The interpretation and revelation came later. I believe we all have been given what's called, "Warning signs" or "Premonitions." It doesn't always come in a dream or vision. When I developed and nurtured my relationship with God, the deeper the revelation became.

I ignored the warning of my dream that day in 2009. Later, I ignored many other warnings. For years, I found myself in a toxic marriage. It was verbal, emotional, psychological, and sometimes physically abusive. Never in a million years would

I have thought I would have reached such a debilitating low. It was almost paralyzing. At times, it felt like it was too much to bare. I am thankful today that through God, I can be transparently, "Nude." I am able to share my life's "Mourning" in all its truth. My pain, highs, lows, nakedness, joy, and hope of continued healing, have been revealed. It is my desire that through my story, others are set free! This is the good news of mourning and being nude.

In writing this book I found great peace in Romans 5:1-5 *"Therefore, since we have been justified by faith, we have peace with God through our Lord Jesus Christ. Through him we have also obtained access by faith into this grace in which we stand, and we rejoice in hope of the glory of God. Not only that, but we rejoice in our sufferings, knowing that suffering produces endurance, and endurance produces character, and character produces hope, and hope does not put us to shame, because God's love has been poured into our hearts through the Holy Spirit who has been given to us."* I could no longer hide or be ashamed of my story. Not only did God free me from that relationship/marriage, he also healed me in so many other areas of my life. We can't help others in areas we have not gone through.

Grief and depression is sometimes out of our control, but it can all produce great fruit. This brings a powerful scripture to mind in Jeremiah 17:8 *"They are like trees planted along a riverbank, with roots that reach deep into the water. Such trees are not bothered by the heat or worried by long months of drought. Their leaves stay green, and they never stop producing fruit.* We all can produce great fruit from our circumstances.

My purpose for writing this book is to share my personal journey through domestic violence, grief, and depression. I am also calling attention to generational trauma. I overcame many obstacles, through prayer, faith, fasting, and surrendering to God's will and purpose. It required me to exercise my faith in my Savior, Jesus Christ. The power and strength of the Lord empowered me. I am in no way perfect which is why I have had many slips and falls. At times, I seriously battled my emotions. At the end of the day, what's important is that I kept fighting. I survived it all and able to tell about it. I am still standing. Every day I am becoming stronger. Welcome to Good Mourning Nude! My personal memoir.

Prayer:

Heavenly Father, we thank you for the precious gift of the Holy Spirit. The Holy Spirit that lives discreetly within us. The gentleness of the spirit that comes to lead, guide and direct our paths. The great comforter that sends us warnings, promptings, and even interpretations about things that we need direction and guidance for. We want to hear from you, Oh Lord, today and every day. As we turn the pages of this book, speak to each reader. Bring about healing and deliverance for their minds, body and soul. With all power and truth of the Holy Trinity.

Amen!

Chapter Two

Family Ties
Generationally Picked

Exodus 20:5 (NLT)

"You must not bow down to them or worship them, for I, the LORD your God, am a jealous God who will not tolerate your affection for any other gods. I lay the sins of the parents upon their children; the entire family is affected--even children in the third and fourth generations of those who reject me."

Domestic violence and depression can flow through generational lineage. The effects of "generational trauma" forms patterns in our family history and bloodlines.

When I was a little girl, my mother was a single parent. She worked a lot of different shifts at the local hospital. For this reason, I spent a lot of time at my maternal grandparent's house. It wasn't the typical grandparent home. I can imagine for a lot of little children, going to the grands meant getting spoiled, eating good food, and doing fun stuff. Maybe we would hang with grandpa in the garage. He would be working on an old classic car. Inside, grandma would allow us to help fix dinner. She'd teach us how to make homemade cookies or cakes from scratch. In a perfect world, grandma and grandpa would keep us safe and out of harm's way. That wasn't the story at my grandparent's home.

There had been a lot of abuse at their house throughout the years. By the time I came into the world things had calmed down. However, the effects of the trauma were residual. Thank God, I was shielded from most of the abuse.

I witnessed alcohol abuse and there was an extreme level of oppression and depression in the atmosphere. When I was between the ages of two and nine I was not able to recognize oppression and depression. I could identify joy, happiness, peace and love. What I recall and witnessed, as a child was a dark home with the curtains drawn closed. It was like night and day in comparison when grandpa was home versus when he wasn't.

Grandma appeared to be tense and nervous when he was there. She wasn't like her relaxed, fun and free self when he wasn't. I could be loud and energetic when he wasn't home but had to be quiet as a church mouse when he was.

I witnessed some of the beatings my mother's younger siblings experienced and the extreme punishments. I saw lack because of economic irresponsibility due to alcohol abuse. What I remember most is that my grandmother suffered from depression. She would have what appeared to me as high and low days.

Years before I was born, grandma was exposed to verbal and physical abuse. Because of the abuse, she suffered a severe head trauma. It came from the beatings she endured. Later, she was diagnosed as a Manic Depressant (now known as Bipolar Disorder) and Schizophrenia. Not fully comprehending her challenges, I thought it was the coolest thing to sit and listen to her. She would share stories or ramblings as different 'characters. Eventually, it would be known as, "episodes" to our family.

There were days that I would come over and she would be none responsive. She would sit in a chair by a wall in the living room for hours looking at television or out of the front door. My grandmother would smoke multiple packs of cigarettes a day. She'd eat and drink a ton of sugary drinks and candy. Her emotional eating and smoking were to escape or cope with her pain. This was one of the many faces of depression. Just being around that environment, I believe planted seeds that I wasn't even aware of. However, these experiences would later play a part in my purpose towards breaking generational inhabitants.

By the time I was a pre-teen my mother had relocated us to St. Louis, Missouri. I got in to trouble quite a bit when I was a teen. That lead to me being put on punishments. I remember isolating myself in my room because I felt like the world was ending! I didn't have access to television, the telephone or my friends. In my mind there was nothing else to do but go to sleep. Sleeping my punishment away seemed like the right way to handle the situation. It was also an attempt to manipulate my mother into giving me less time on the punishment. The only problem was, I would sleep for hours at a time all to wake up and still be on punishment. So, I would go back to sleep.

The only one I was really hurting was myself. The real question is, "why was I so troubled as a youth?" When brokenness and rebellion show up, its usually because something is going on in the inside or in one's environment. It's an inward cry for outward help. We see this in society every day. Depression and grief are very much like that short sleep pattern from day to day. You will feel the same way if you don't address adverse situations or circumstance. Your will and drive are gravely dormant.

My way of dealing with issues was nurturing an unhealthy pattern of behavior. I should have handled it in a more constructive way, like reading or writing. I am sure part of it was my immaturity and pride. A huge part was because I didn't know how. At times, I could not express myself. Therefore, patterns and behaviors formed that I would carry into my adulthood.

My mother later shared, by the time I had reached my teenage years, she was battling a very sullen depression. She had gone through some difficult challenges in her life which lead to unhappiness and grief. Like some, she was functionally depressed. Mom, went to work every day, cared for me, and took care of our home. She also had a lot of what she would call "vegging out" time. This had become her temporary escape route. This equated to zoning out with unhealthy snacks, lying on the coach, and watching countless hours of television. I believe stressful events at work, parenting a difficult teenager, and past unresolved family dysfunction were figuratively eating away at her. She was now dealing with challenges like her mother did.

Those generational patterns and behaviors were recycling. I learned that my maternal great-grandmother also suffered from depression and other vices. The same holds true for many of my family members who have suffered from some form of trauma or dysfunction. They fought off strongholds such as anxiety, poverty, illnesses, domestic violence, and addictions. We have the power to overcome these things, less they become generational patterns and behaviors.

In my dream where the enemy was there because of the familiar ailments, an "Invitation" was given. What I gave power to, had the power to take me out. I had to start breaking the cycle of being generationally picked. It was necessary to move past simply "breaking" generational curses, but rather "destroying" generational trauma. What is broken can also be put back together. A broken vase can be put back together with all the pieces and some good glue. A broken heart can be mended over time with patience and healing. I had to learn to let go of fear, anxiety, worry, pain, hurt and other traumas. Those issues were paralyzing me. It has not been easy. Trust me. I know. That is why I am sharing my journey and my heart.

The scripture in the beginning of the chapter enlightens us. God will "lay" the sins of the parents' down upon their children—third and fourth generation. There is an advanced study in epigenetics. The word "lay" denotes the path and course of future and current generations being affected by the decisions and choices made by the lineage of parents. It further shows that generational trauma can be scientifically traced back from one generation to another. It reveals that our life experiences and choices change us.

Changes move through our brain and down to our DNA level. These changes can be passed onto our children and further down the hereditary line. Epigenetics gives insight into how our diet, work, environment, and traumatic events can change the genetic legacy we pass onto our children and grandchildren. Neurology scientific researchers define Epigenetics as information that sits above the genome. It controls the programming of DNA. It instructs different cells how to express themselves.

In an interview from the "Conquer Series", a new men's DVD-based teaching series, neuropsychologist, Dr. Jes Montgomery explains, sensations we put into the brain will use the DNA to change how the cell responds. Those genes are turned off or on based on what that response is. The DNA doesn't change, the expression does. What's fascinating about this new study is, it reveals that our DNA is not immutable. That was the former notion, but that environment markedly affects our gene expressions and the ways we function and behave.

Exodus 20:5 says, *"You shall not bow down to them or worship them, for I, the Lord God, am a jealous God, punishing the children for the sin of the parents to the third and fourth generation of those who hate me. Having wisdom to know and discern that sins can give birth to sin, hardships and pain."*

Challenges occur that are unexplainable. In those instances, we have to trust the process of our existence and faith to lead us to a greater purpose. Romans 8:28 encourages, *"And we know that in all things God works for the good of those who love him, who have been called according to his purpose."*

I believe science and spiritual intelligence can bring clarity and understanding of generational patterns. It shows that we can play an active role in breaking away from and through its enchainment of our minds. The issues that affect our thinking, emotions, reactions, and will. We should not be so quick to categorize someone because of their actions or situation. We should exam the root cause of a person's behavior or pattern.

I have outlined some ways that have helped me to recognize and destroy the cycle of generational inhabitants. I truly hope that these nine highlights will assist you in the undertaking of your own battles and infirmities.

1. Recognize the Curse: Research you and your partner or spouse's family lineage, maternal and paternal. Identify patterns of sins and struggles they have practiced or indulged in. Own and acknowledge sin in your own life that you have been challenged with. Knowing and acknowledging this information can help derail patterns and behaviors that may try to infiltrate your family.

2. Fasting, Giving, Praying: I have learned over the years through the Word of God and by experience that fasting is a necessity in our lives. Fasting is a secret source of power and helps to build our spiritual and physical strength. It nurtures the intimate relationship with God. When you have a relationship with God, you have access to breakthroughs, answers, directions, intentional peace, and love.

Giving moves you beyond yourself to think of others that are in need or that should be appreciated. Not only do I give in tithes and offering to my church, I give to the community.

Praying is vital to our connection and relationship with God. It draws us closer in conversations with Him. Prayer is not all about getting your prayers answered or petitions heard. It is also being in tune with God and the Holy Spirit as you listen for His voice and direction.

a. Matthew 6:6-7 *"But when you pray, go into your room, close the door and pray to your Father, who is unseen. Then your Father, who sees what is done in secret, will reward you.*

And when you pray, do not keep on babbling like pagans, for they think they will be heard because of their many words."

b. *Matthew 6:18 "so that it will not be obvious to others that you are fasting, but only to your Father, who is unseen; and your Father, who sees what is done in secret, will reward you."*

3. Destroy the Curse: Apply God's Word and power over your life. Choose to walk in righteousness and obedience to God. The chains of bondage shall not only be broken, but also destroyed.

a. Give your life to Jesus. The blood of Jesus removes our sin (atonement for our sins) 1 John 2:2 *"He himself is the sacrifice that atones for our sins and not only our sins but the sins of all the world."*

b. Fight the battle with spiritual, not carnal weapons. Put on the full armor of God. Ephesians 6:12 *"For we are not fighting against flesh-and-blood enemies, but against evil rulers and authorities of the unseen world, against mighty powers in this dark world, and against evil spirits in the heavenly places."* Speak life and not death over your situation and arm yourself with God's word.

    c. Exercise self-control by using willpower. The ability to say "No." Proverbs 21:23 *"He who guards his mouth and his tongue, guards his soul from troubles."*

    4. Reverse the Curse: Live free and victoriously.

    a. Recognize your enemy. We battle not against flesh and blood. Our enemy is in the things that we do and say that are contradictory to the word and power of God. The battle is spiritual. Ephesians 6:11 *"Put on the full armor of God, so that you can be able to stand firm against the schemes of the adversary."*

    b. Forgive people who have hurt you. Matthew 6:14 (ISV) *"For if you forgive people of their offenses, your heavenly Father will also forgive you."*

    5. Address the Root Cause of the Curse and not the Symptom: (ex: jealousy, envy, gossip, fear, insecurity). Proverbs 4:23 (NLT*) "Guard your heart above all else, for it determines the course of your life."*

    6. Release the Power of Love: Unconditional love will release blessings. To truly understand the Love of God in your life, you must love those who hurt you, those who sinned against you, and those who have opposed you. Honestly, God is STILL working on me in this area. I am getting better daily. It's toxic to hold onto. 1 Corinthians 13:13 *"And now these three remain: faith, hope and love. But the greatest of these is love."*

7. Have a Sincere Godly Attitude: Our attitude determines our outcome. Proverbs 17:22 *"A joyful heart is good medicine, but a crushed spirit dries up the bones."*

8. Aligning our Words and Actions with God's Words: Our words give evidence and proof of our faith and activates the power to change. Ephesians 2:18 *"For through Him we both have access by one Spirit to the Father."*

9. Receive God's Love & Acceptance: We do not have to live a life full of pain, hurt, shame or sadness. God's love and acceptance is so much greater than anything. It's hard at times to fathom a love so pure and powerful, but it does exist. Just ask and receive it. John 3:16 *"For God so loved the world, that he gave his only begotten Son, that whosoever believeth in him should not perish, but have everlasting life."*

10. Obedience is greater than Sacrifice: We have to learn to walk in God's freedom. Through obedience and by surrendering our will to His will and His way we can be free. Our decisions to hear and obey, affects and determines our future. If we deny those things that keep us in bondage, it is the very thing that holds us captive and the inability to fly free. 2 Samuel 24:24 *"But the king replied to Araunah, 'No, I insist on paying you for it. I will not sacrifice to the Lord my God burnt offerings that cost me nothing.'"*

Don't allow your families or others dysfunction to keep you from being who you are predestined to be. You have been created for greatness!

"Do not allow traumatic events in your life to paralyze your movement and stunt your growth!"

Author Unknown

Prayer:

Lord, we thank you for your knowledge and truth of your Word that sets us free. Thank you for showing us the root causes of our problems and generational challenges. Thank you for your strength that is made perfect in our weakness. For the ability and desire to change our ways and our mindsets. This way we can live free, healthy, and whole lives. Help us start each day by acknowledging your presence and plans for our lives and begin to take steps in the right direction. We ask that you lift the heaviness from our hearts and minds. Heaviness that makes us feel as though we can't be released from the hands of our adversaries. May the works and the plans of the enemy be destroyed! May we smile with your strength and live with your grace. In Jesus Christ name we pray.

Amen!

Chapter Three

Controlled Conversations
(Peek-A-Boo Private)

Luke 14:28 ESV

"For which of you, desiring to build a tower, does not first sit down and count the cost, whether he has enough to complete it?"

I'll never forget the time, my maternal grandmother said, "Maury, if you don't want your business told then you shouldn't tell it!" As far back as I can remember, my family has always been very private. We were selective about who we shared intimate business with. One of my close friends and I used to laugh as we recalled a family member saying, "Don't nobody care about your business. You think people always worried about your business." This was coming from someone who was always wanting to know everyone's business. This person also hated to be left out, and was just as private, if not secretive about their own life.

There is an old saying, *"Everyone notices everyone else's problems but never pay attention to their own."*
Jerrett Parker

Family secrets, dysfunctions, and wounds were not discussed or disclosed most times. If they were discussed, decades would have passed before the issues were revisited. It was difficult opening up and sharing with family members. It was even harder sharing the dark places with those who were sometimes not relatives. Looking back, I realize, it wasn't necessarily alliances built on loyalty and trust. It often stemmed from shame and pride. Don't ask and don't tell didn't start with the United States military. In my opinion, it started inside the homes of many families. But why?

I remember when I met my ex-husband, he was vaguely and selectively private. He told stories that were "safe" and "humorous" to be retold. We all have those stories, right? You remember that one time when Uncle Cliff got so stoned that he drove his car into his own house? He believed his wife was inside sleeping with his son's baseball coach. What about when your grandfather was a PIMP and use to walk his girls down the street with dog collars on? You know those stories that are so far removed that the embarrassment and possibility of shame has subsided. Perhaps it wasn't your story. That made it okay to tell others and laugh about it.

There were untold stories that were not shared prior to marrying my ex-husband. Truths on his side about the history of neglect, physical, mental, and emotional abuse in his childhood were not shared. The neglect or mistreatment of siblings by the parent(s) or times of anger and rage were not a footnote. He failed to mention the affection and attention that lacked in the home. The source of co-dependency that allowed all those things to happen, seized to be revealed. Those challenges were never shared even after we were married. However, scars can only hide for so long. Over time, the bare essence of those scars were exposed. When I was younger, my mother would say "What goes on in the dark will eventually come to the light."

I believe that in any relationship, friend or courtship, one has the right to full disclosure. Individuals should have the right to know who they are involved with. They should know what they are signing up for. I have always been a private person. However, who I believed was my lifelong partner and best friend, I was a lot more open with my truths and family history. In fact, my ex-husband was able to see for himself in many ways. He was around my entire network of friends and family. However, my vulnerability and naivety backfired on me over the years in that relationship. I signed up with someone that seemed to be genuine and trust-worthy.

However, scars can only hide for so long. Over time, the bare essence of those scars were exposed. Reiterating what my mother said, "What goes on in the dark will eventually come to the light." Man, was that ever a true statement!

Many, many times I probably shared too much since I held so much in other times. Now I felt safe to share and release. I don't believe my ex was comfortable or secure in who he was. In many ways neither was I. What I later discovered was that my ex presented me with the "representation" of what he "thought" he should possibly or wanted to be. Sometimes, people are just not comfortable with being themselves. They fear that others may not like them. They also may be afraid of losing that person. When people hide who they are, it can lead to great disappointment and loss of trust. In some instances, it can lead to life-altering changes. Covering up the truth or withholding information that is necessary to share can hurt or damage someone.

Each person is equally responsible for doing their due diligence. Asking questions, researching, and checking backgrounds of individuals is important. This is especially vital if you are choosing to join with someone for life! Something that I did not do until years later; years too late, years later! What's in the lineage of someone's family and history is vital to a person's future and to their life! 1 Peter 5:8 *"Be of sober spirit, be on the alert. Your adversary, the devil, prowls about like a roaring lion, seeking someone to devour."* Scripture says, "devour." There are attacks on our lives that come from the adversary through generational assignments and despondency. The devil comes to kill, steal, and destroy. If you are not free in your mind and heart, you are not free to be who God has called you to be. This lack of freedom and truth or lack of, can manifest into toxic behaviors and deceitful thinking.

I have been guilty of sharing with my girlfriends, family or associates what I wanted them to know about me or my circumstances. However, nothing to trick, fool or hurt someone. There is a difference. For me, it was extraordinarily hard for me to walk and live in my imperfect truth at times. I was afraid to live in my truth. Deep down, I struggled with rejection. I had gone through so much hurt and disappointment. I did not want people to know the deep dark places of my imperfections. However, I could only hide for so long. My truths ultimately came crashing down around and inside of me.

One of my truths that I was holding on to and I was hiding was that fact that I was in an abusive marriage. This truth kept me from knowing myself. It silenced me in shame, guilt, and fear. I was only hurting myself and my children by not seeking help sooner. The truth began to unfold in my appearance, lack of happiness, resources, finances, and mental health. I became unstable in areas that I had always been stable in. I questioned myself. There were times I was mad at myself for not seeing or wanting to see the red flags. What my ex didn't share with me was eventually revealed by his close family members. They empathized with my pain. I believe God put it on their hearts to tell the truth.

The truth of controlled conversations and hidden trauma. It was his hidden truth that literally almost destroyed me and my children. Ultimately, his truth led me on a desperate path of searching both of our families hidden truths. It has been in my desolate wilderness journey to be free. This way I too discovered the epigenetic path that lead me to this place. I had to get real with myself and those around me. This was important if I was going to change the generational path of my children. I needed to move from controlling conversations to conscious conversations.

DISCERNING GODLY COUNSEL

There were many times out of a mentally emotional space that I would become vulnerable. In my moments of disappointment and hurt, I would move from being peek-a-boo private to sharing more than I should have with the wrong person (s). Proverbs 11:14 tells us, *"Where there is no counsel, the people fall but in the multitude of counselors there is safety."*

There is a huge price to pay when we share with the wrong people. In matters of life and death situations, we should value and respect that our life is made up of good and bad choices. When we are dealing with life-altering situations, we have to be careful about who we allow to impart into us. For me, I was desperate for spiritual intuitiveness and Godly wisdom. Sometimes, without harmful intentions, people can get wrapped up in the world's advice, contradictions and promises. We can think, react, and respond like the world. However, there are times that God will use the world. He will send a message or revelation to us through them. He can do whatever He wants.

There were times in my own life when the realization and importance of discernment became clear. It directed me to a place where I could no longer afford to seek or have worldly or wrong advice given. I became so hungry and desperate to be whole and free. All I had was God and His word. What I allowed to be downloaded into my mind and spirit had to be safeguarded. I needed people committed to PRAYING for me not PREYING on the drama in my life. The kind of drama that would make my business the front-page news of gossip. I didn't need my circumstances being used for someone else's unhappy and unfulfilled world. I too have fallen prey to gossip.

It's something about pain that drives you to change! It's sad when our own insecurities and deflections shine a spotlight on someone else's imperfections. This is to validate why we are not perfect inside. Yet, we are not willing to share the truth or root-cause of what our unhappiness or discontent is. For me, this had to change. I had to walk through the process and offense when people just wanted to be nosey and then move on. I can't tell you how many times I've had conversations with people or organizations that I thought cared or could help. Unfortunately, they didn't or couldn't help me.

It started to become traumatizing and exhausting, sharing with the wrong people. I made a change. It brought about the resources, friends, counsel, and mentors that God had specifically aligned and assigned to my life. They came during a time when I needed to walk the path of healing and wholeness. The bridge that God built in my personal relationship with him created a stronger mind and stronger discernment. I began dedicating alone time in prayer and meditation with Him. By reading my bible, listening to wise and godly counsel, the assignment became clearer. I had to get in a spiritual posture. Then position myself to hear and to receive step by step instructions. It was critical to my faith, my growth, my life!

For my children and I to heal, be safe and evolve I had to abandon the peek-a-boo private pattern. James 1:16-18 *"Do not be deceived, my beloved brothers. Every good and perfect gift is from above, coming down from the Father of the heavenly lights, with whom there is no change or shifting shadow. He chose to give us birth through the word of truth, that we would be a kind of first fruits of His creation."* When we hide what we are dealing with, those things have the potential to destroy us. Walking in our truth and imperfections allows us to become stronger and wiser. Those truths can possibly even save someone's life. I'm a witness. It has saved my own.

I believe what my grandmother told me that day had some truth to it. I now see with a different set of lenses, "If you don't want your business to circle back to do more harm, cause greater disappointment and fuel lack of trust, then seek wise and Godly counsel. It should come from those that God has aligned and assigned to you in those moments. When you need help, healing and to hear the truth in love they are there." I have learned that growing through what I have gone through, my help comes in many forms. That help is meant to assist and not hinder.

The truth about where we are today may look bleak and scary as to what tomorrow holds. I have often times found myself staring into my past. I'm praising God for how far I have come. Stop hiding and burying those things that you need to face. Deal with it in order to be free mentally, emotionally and spiritually! Remember always that God's Love lives Free!

Prayer:

Heavenly Father, we kill the enemy of lies, deception, fear, rejection, and doubt of the ability of oneself. We face our adversary that was sent to kill, steal, and destroy us. We ask that you give or restore within us, love, truth, peace, hope, freedom, comfort, and joy. May we walk free and boldly into your promises for our loved ones and ourselves. May we not be a stumbling block or hindrances to ourselves or those around us. May we authentically captivate, touch, and inspire those around us to live a life free of secrets and pain, but a life of liberty and wholeness. In your son's name Jesus Christ, we ask and pray.

Amen!

Part 2

UNCOVERED WOUNDS

2 CORINTHIANS 12:7-10

"And lest I should be exalted above measure through the abundance of the revelations, there was given to me a thorn in the flesh, the messenger of Satan to buffet me, lest I should be exalted above measure. For this thing I besought the Lord thrice, that it might depart from me. And he said unto me, My grace is sufficient for thee: for my strength is made perfect in weakness. Most gladly therefore will I rather glory in my infirmities, that the power of Christ may rest upon me. Therefore, I take pleasure in infirmities, in reproaches, in necessities, in persecutions, in distresses for Christ's sake: for when I am weak, then am I strong."

Chapter Four

Into Darkness
The Abyss of Depression

Job 12:22

"He uncovers the deeps out of darkness and brings deep darkness to light."

50

I remember the first time I admitted to someone and myself that I struggled with depression. I traveled through so many emotions about my marriage, life, loss, and disappointments. It's like it just hit me one day, "I'm depressed." I could no longer hide from it. I looked around at my environment, my energy, and the vibrations that I was giving off. It was sometimes very daunting and negative due to the oppressive atmosphere in my personal life. It was like trying to break a bad habit or quit an addiction. In this case, this habit or addiction had a stronger hold on me than I wanted to confess.

During this time, my friends and family would tell me how proud of me that they were. They would also tell me how strong I was. My favorite was, "girl I don't even worry about you. No matter what you go through, you always bounce back." Somehow this time, what they didn't know was, every day was a struggle. I felt like the important things in my life were literally slipping through my hands. There were times, I would see my children off to school in the morning. I would then draw the curtains. Next, I would get a bunch of junk food and lay on the couch. Then I would watch endless hours of Netflix or just sleep. Each day, it became harder for me to even raise my head above the pillows. I would dread daylight coming or the sun rising. I would wake up in the wee hours of the morning hating to see 3:30, 4:15, or 5:45a.m. It was then that I knew my hiding in the darkness was approaching sunlight. The fact that I had to face yet another day of responsibilities. I would have to be a mom, a wife separated from her spouse, provider, business woman, friend, or daughter. The thought of being anything just was exhausting. I just wanted to be alone all the time. Truth is, there were some days that I just wanted the good Lord above to call me home. I didn't even have the courage to commit suicide. The thought of enduring any more pain, pained me! Horrible right? That's my truth!

In my depression, I would day dream about pioneers. Fore-runners who had left the earth but at one time were significant in my life. I would dream of conversations, the joy that we would have. They were whisked away from life as we once knew it. Envy pumped through my veins at times, feeling like they had been chosen. They left their responsibilities and abandon their cares but really, they had passed on. I realized how very selfish it was of me. I knew that my children would not only miss me but that they needed and depended on me. They enjoyed me, and I enjoyed them. In fact, it was my children that kept me going every single day.

My daughter was old enough to realize that something didn't seem quite right. The nurturing spirit that she was, began to really worry about me. She would try to keep me encouraged. It was refreshing at times and felt like a ray of sunshine peering inside a dark cave. I also felt a great deal of guilt behind it. How could I allow her to see this side of me? Why wasn't I capable of being strong like everyone expected me to be? Better yet, the person they thought I was? How did I allow myself to reach this low place to sink in and change the energy of my thinking? My daughter was at a very pivotal time in her life. She was quickly approaching her senior year of high school. Embracing the next chapter of her life at University and becoming an adult should have been her focus. I had to be the one to support her financially, emotionally, and spiritually.

It was difficult for my son to understand the separation between his father and I. He was so young and one of few words and speech. The 14-year age difference between my two children required that I parent/minister to them differently. Who had time to be damn depressed? But I was hurting, afraid, and lonely. I felt so insignificant. I was grieving, hurting, and in an abyss of darkness.

Something about that low place was also very sobering, and eye-opening. I realized that I moved past people every day in traffic, the office, at school, the coffee shop, shopping mall, dentist office, in the elevator, at a park, the gas station or the gym. These people were desperate, lonely, broken and hurting individuals. Some people you could see it by the way that they dressed. You could tell others by the way the inside of their homes looked. You could also tell by the inside of their vehicles or just by looking into their eyes. Then there were many people who had become quite good at pretending or masking. The fake persona of what they wanted us to believe, "that everything was ok."

There are men, women, and children who mask the characteristic of abuse and depression every day. Yet, these individuals are facing abuse in their love relationships, home, or families. People mask addiction and dysfunctional behaviors. Life is moving at such an accelerated pace. At times, we are too busy to notice someone else's pain. Sometimes it's simply because we are caught up in our own entanglements. Other times we see it, but too afraid to approach it or get involved.

For decades, I had been the listening ear for many. Now I was finding myself needing to vent, talk, release. It made me feel very inadequate. Part of my depression, if I can be honest, was that I too was holding myself as much a hostage as my circumstances. I could not stay out of my mind or my thoughts.

It was as if I had been holding my breath underwater with no hope of getting air. Not realizing, all I needed to do was lift my head. There was air, sun, and hope ready to greet me. That day, I spoke to a close friend about my depression. It was shortly after that God revealed this book to me. However, it wasn't just about the depression. It was also about the questions that would follow. Why was I depressed? Who caused this depression? Where did this great sense of loss come from?

Depression was merely the stronghold and the result of what was taunting me. I remembered hearing something once about going through life's trials and tribulations. I remember someone saying something like, "Sometimes you just have to sit in it to feel it." At first it seemed very callous and insensitive. As time went on, I realized that to some degree of what I was living through, I had to survive and change my thinking. In order to remit, I had to first admit. I was believing the lies and walking in the insecurities of a very broken mindset and spirit.

Stemming from childhood, I never believed that I was enough for myself. I also did not think I was enough for the right partner and friendships to love. I was living in fear of being alone. Over the course of time, I had been broken down. Now, I was starting to believe that I would never be able to rebuild and support myself again. I was in my own head, blaming myself for being in bondage and oppression. I had overwhelming doubt that the God I believed in would send a rescue team for me. I just simply started to lose hope in anything and everything.

My circumstances seemed to be getting worse and more dangerous. Somehow, I clung to the little faith and hope in God I still had. I drew strength from stories in the bible or others that survived similar circumstances and hardships. There were stories that I was able to personally identify with. I saw the transformative power of why God led me to these specific people. He orchestrated these moments and stories for me to draw strength and renewed trust. I could relate to many bible stories, but a few in particularly gave me peace, hope and strength;

- **The story of Job:** Perseverance through trials, testing and remaining faithful to God will help you make it. A newfound faith is birthed through trials and tribulations. When we have to sit in it. (Job chapters 1-42)

- **The story of Joseph:** A slave became one who saves, never losing hope when faced with many challenges. Joseph was still God's favored. He had a plan for Joseph and his family's life all along. (Genesis chapters 37-50)

- **The story of Hannah:** Hope and strength were gained through fervent prayers to God. Despite what people may say, think or ridicule you over, God will show up on time and silences the naysayers. (1 Samuel chapters 1-2)

- **The story of Shadrach, Meshach and Abednego:** Stand on what you believe and trust God, no matter how hot the heat gets turned up in your life. God is faithful to bring you out. (Daniel chapter 3)

I pray that you will take the time to read these individuals stories. May peace and comfort surround you. It is my hope that by sharing my personal journey, you will be enlightened and empowered.

Over time I started to FIGHT against my depression, spiritually, mentally, physically, and holistically. I am not a licensed therapist or medical doctor. Everyone's situation and circumstances are different. I am a huge advocate of healthy HELP. Whatever shape or form that may be for each individual. At the end the day, we have to take the necessary steps to aid ourselves to wellness. If that means using all the steps outlined below in conjunction with medical advice or adopting some or none of the outlined suggestions. Whatever gets you to feeling God's absolute best is what I pray and hope for. I have been to what felt like rock bottom. It was a very scary and real place for me. My heart and ministry is to share routines and faith practices that I nurtured and developed. These things got me to a healthy and peaceful landing place.

How I BATTLED through Domestic Violence & Depression:

- I started eating healthy:
  o Cutting out sugar, eating less carbohydrates, drinking lots of alkaline water, less juice
  o Eating more healthy green vegetables, overall fresh fruits and raw or cooked vegetables
  o Freshly cooked food and less processed foods
  o Plenty of fiber and protein
- I started exercising 4-5 days a week and I did different activities, so I wouldn't get bored with the routine:
  o Hot Bikram Yoga
  o Bike Riding (Cycling)
  o Aqua Fitness Classes
  o Swimming
  o Gym Workout (Treadmill, Weights, Classes, Etc.)
- Audiobooks on the Bible which I would find specific stories of individuals who had experienced or gone

through what I may have been facing; depression, loss, betrayal, grieving, etc. (Example: King David Old Testament Stories, The book of Job, The story of Joseph in Genesis, Naomi in the book of Ruth)

- I found time to relax by the pool, the beach, closing my eyes in my parked car, thinking of a beautiful place, treating myself to a foot or hand massage. Reflexology.
- Each day was a process. I started by simply taking one step at a time. Putting one foot in front of the other. Taking one day at a time.
- I would search out other positive readings and positive media searches. (If you are to read, listen, or watch anything make sure it's positive and uplifting, especially during this time while your mind is so fragile)
- I stayed away from alcohol, drugs and other toxins like tobacco, sugar, carbs and environments and people that participated in those things.
- I had to start bridling my tongue.   While I was down, I had become so negative and pessimistic. I started getting on my own nerves. I'm convinced those who were closet around me (what they must've endured…lol). So, you have to "Guard your tongue. Be careful what you speak out of your mouth. Positive words and speech challenge."

- I journaled my thoughts and dreams a lot via email, audio notes, electronic notepad, or good ole pen and paper.
- I did deep level spiritual healing and deliverance counseling, I wrote two books!!! I Tried Hypnosis Therapy Consultation. That was interesting…. lol.
- I never stopped praying. Even if it was just a few words that I could utter, "Lord help me!"
- I wrote out Power Scriptures/ God's Promises.
- I wrote out powerful affirmations and put them on the wall of my office in my home. I tried to speak over myself, daily. I confessed positive affirmations about myself: i.e. "I am strong and not weak," "I am thoughtful, powerful and loved,"
- I wrote out goals; 1 year and then 5 year (things to plan and strive for)
- I created a bucket list: "Life is Worth Living List" Traveling to a specific country, missions' trip(s), giving to a certain charity, jet skiing, hockey game, finishing my degree, speaking engagements
- I learned to accept loss. Then I sought to discover what role (if any) that I may have played in that loss or disappointment. I had to learn to forgive myself and other parties involved and let go. "The Power of Letting Go." The power of growth.

- I learned to love myself and others: I reached out daily or weekly to tell someone how much I loved, appreciated and adored them. I let them know that I was praying for and listening to them. When we focus on the positive in someone else, it uplifts us. Uplifting and recognizing them as someone important and needed in our lives is valuable. This is not intended for those that intentionally hurt us. Those dysfunctional components in our lives have to be left behind.

- Embrace the season: It's not a lifetime (allowing yourself time to heal). Seasons change, and every problem has an expiration date. When you're going through abuse, grief and depression, it can literally consume you. It can make you feel as if you will never get past that moment—that trauma, that hurt, that pain. It will try to convince you that you will always be where you are in your current situation. This can make you feel stuck or paralyzed. Know that this is not the truth. We have to allow ourselves the proper time to heal. The time will come when the fog, the heaviness, and the weight will be lifted. Be ready to walk from underneath the cloud once it starts to move. It really is a choice! We can learn from everything that we go through. What did you learn? How did you change or grow?

- When I can, I really try to get 6-8 hours of sleep each night. If I can sneak a nap in on the weekends for 30-

60 minutes, then I will. Remember, don't sleep or nap too long. A healthy diet will help with energy levels and help your body feel well rested. If you are unable to get a full 8 hours, sleep or take naps during the day.

- Meditation and breathing: Meditating on God's promises and practice breathing techniques to relieve stress and pressure.

- I stopped tolerating dysfunctional and abusive behavior from my ex-husband and filed for a divorce. I took a huge step to gaining my freedom back.

- I stopped being too nice and naive. Meaning, I am loving and firm in my beliefs. I know who I am and what I want. I now know what I will not stand for. Being too nice and so naïve put me in compromising situations. Those situations almost took my life. Using wisdom and discernment were key for me.

- I started individual counseling for me and my children. I joined a domestic violence support group. I met some amazing women and I was inspired by very compelling stories.

- One of the truths of Domestic Violence is that "Domestic Violence thrives in silence." I began to share my story whenever God would lead me to share with friends and family. However, most times it was with complete strangers. I would find out through sharing, they were going through or had gone through DV themselves.

- Educate yourself. Do your research. I started to research domestic violence, grief and depression. It was through my research that I was able to identify, relate and realize the sobering truth of my situation.
- I started to focus on the "END." The end of the story or the battle I envisioned me winning. Despite what it looked like at the beginning or while going through, I had to see the end as Victory! Therefore, I focused on the positive outcome and saw me at the finish line.
- I literally had to retrain my brain and tongue to not think or speak it. Sometimes this simply meant just being quiet if I didn't have anything positive to say.
- Talking it out, to get it out. In a safe space sometimes, I had to.

PRAYER:

Praying Ephesians 6:10-18 (NIV) over myself and now for you. I believe with the armor of God, we can and will come out of darkness;

The Armor of God

"Finally, be strong in the Lord and in his mighty power. Put on the full armor of God, so that you can take your stand against the devil's schemes. For our struggle is not against flesh and

blood, but against the rulers, against the authorities, against the powers of this dark world and against the spiritual forces of evil in the heavenly realms. Therefore, put on the full armor of God, so that when the day of evil comes, you may be able to stand your ground, and after you have done everything, to stand. Stand firm then, with the belt of truth buckled around your waist, with the breastplate of righteousness in place, and with your feet fitted with the readiness that comes from the gospel of peace. In addition to all this, take up the shield of faith, with which you can extinguish all the flaming arrows of the evil one. Take the helmet of salvation and the sword of the Spirit, which is the word of God. And pray in the Spirit on all occasions with all kinds of prayers and requests. With this in mind, be alert and always keep on praying for all the Lord's people."

Amen

Chapter Five

Baring Disappointment

Isaiah 40:28-31 (ESV)

Have you not known? Have you not heard?
The Lord is the everlasting God,
the Creator of the ends of the earth.
He does not faint or grow weary;
his understanding is unsearchable.
He gives power to the faint,
and to him who has no might he increases strength.
Even youths shall faint and be weary,
and young men shall fall exhausted;
but they who wait for the Lord shall renew their strength;
they shall mount up with wings like eagles;
they shall run and not be weary;
they shall walk and not faint.

How does one really face or even accept disappointment? How does your body or your brain act or react to countless disappointments? I am speaking of major life-altering disappointments like a divorce, low to no income, going from A+ credit to being buried in debt. How do you handle disappointing situations? Surrendering your home and vehicle or becoming a party in a lawsuit, causes public humiliation. You are in a major car accident and your car gets totaled-out. Theft, betrayal, death of friends or family are major disappointments. When you're close to homelessness, living out of a hotel for weeks, and your career is threatened, that's major. Your sanity-challenged, and your strength tested. You know, the type of disappointments and setbacks that shake and rock you to the core. That shake that will have you feeling out of sorts. That disappointment that literally rocks, shifts, or changes who or what you are.

Funny thing about disappointments is that it doesn't send a text, e-mail, or a D.M. to say that it's coming. It just shows up! Yes, perhaps there are those things or people that you may have been pre-warned about. As a result, disappointment happened. What about the disappointments that has a snow ball effect? One after another and you had no clue that it was coming and how to handle it?

For what felt like an extended time, I metaphorically was standing in a batting cage with the lights out. The balls where coming at me at an accelerated speed. I was trying to swat whatever I could to prevent the balls from hitting me. Disappointment became an understatement when issues in my life were coming at me like a wrecking ball. This had become my new normal. Most days I was just going through the motions. Later, I realized that I was not even processing what was happening.

I believe disappointment is connected to grief. To get through it, you have to process it. I am not speaking of just going through the process or the motions. One must, actually break down the events that has transpired. Sometimes you have to sit in it, to feel it, so that it marinates change. Whether it is loss, a missed opportunity or trust broken, you might feel it. When you have the expectation of something turning out one way but ended up another, sit in it. These are all situations and occurrences to process.

Processing disappointments, I've learned to start with the elements of Who, What, When, Where and Why. These key components allow us to gather all the information that we need to think logically and rationally. So many people deal with disappointment much like depression or loss. They bury it deep down inside and overlook the elements needed to process the pain. I've been guilty of this myself. I would suppress the hurt and disappointment. Meanwhile, I was slowly chipping away inside.

Over time, I started to recognize this about myself. Before I learned to process things, I would suppress my disappointments and hide my true struggles. I was becoming completely aloof of things happening around me and to me. It was overwhelming and mind-boggling. How could I have even reached such a low level of disappointment and pain? I questioned God in every way. It was like I shook my fist to him for what was happening in me and my children's lives. I was a woman who prayed for many individuals and families for decades. Now it seemed as though my prayers weren't even reaching the outer crest of the earth's realm. They most certainly could not have made it to the heavenly portal to God's ear.

I questioned everything in my past at that point. Every wrong choice, judgment, transgression, and missed opportunity were questioned. Helping others and acts of kindness were not far behind. I lumped them all together in the name of Karma. It wasn't Karma though. It was LIFE. The disappointments of life. More importantly, it was my journey to spiritual maturity. It was the road to becoming whole and free. It was the road to my destiny and purpose on this earth. It was the road I discovered to destroying generational assignments and trauma.

I didn't know how to process things, and I certainly didn't recognize the good to come from it in the beginning. I was simply going through what seemed like the process to get to the other side of hard times. I suffered more because of my lack of knowledge and understanding. It took my mother saying to me one day after our prayer time, "Maury, I've been praying that we all learn to process things the way God intends for us to process what we go through in life." This was so reflective for me in that moment. I started to trace all the circumstantial events and situations that had transpired over seven to nine years. I had not been processing those disappointments. I had just been rolling with the punches trying not to be knocked out of the ring.

Most of my life, I seemed to be just going through the motions. This was relating to certain relationships, friendships, environments, and social groups. In some respects, the "go along to get along." This was very much present for the first two and a half plus decades of my existence. I was an individual thinker and innovator. However, I didn't allow myself the patience to elevate and grow as I would have hoped. I now, did not want to look back and have wasted idle time, standing still; figuratively. Some major disappointment and setbacks in my life came from being attached to the wrong people and environments.

There came a new phase or a new level of disappointments. I had financial, career and educational setbacks, legal battles, marital disappointments, parenting mistakes and pains. There were investment blunders and an all-around loss. I endured bereavement spiritually, mentally, physically, financially, and emotionally. It was draining and exhausting most days. Being real with my truth, I had to be willing to acknowledge that I was hurting and disappointed.

My truth wasn't always what I signed up for. Being the only daughter, granddaughter, and niece on my mother's side came with a lot of pressure. I felt I had to always do right, be perfect and take the advice of my elders. I remember when I was about 12 or 13-years-old. My mom sent me to Barbizon modeling and charm school. I was the only African American in my class that summer. I was tall, lanky and awkward like many of the other girls. Still, the questions would fly from other races like, "How did you get your hair like that?" "Why are you so skinny?" "What happened to your teeth?"

The constant stares from my peers and their parents told me that I was different. That caused me to strive extra hard to be my best. It wasn't necessary to fit in, but to show that I could do what was expected of me. However, no modeling or charm school was going to teach me how to deal with what I was battling on the inside. There had to be more than just charm school to show me what self-love and self-confidence was. Charm school wasn't going to shield me from life's disappointments and setbacks.

How we process disappointment can serve as a catalyst for growth and maturity. I have learned to turn my disappointments into personal gain and growth. Recognizing that I should never lose myself or hold onto the pain from circumstances I cannot change! Once I lifted my head out of the sand, I could see each day. The days presented new opportunities for me to rebuild, be free, learn and grow from my experiences. I decided to go back to the fundamentals of *"who, what, when, where and why."*

- Discovering "who" I was
- "What" it was going to take to move forward in "what" I was created for
- Deepening my, "why" of "what" I wanted to accomplish and achieve
- Looking at "where" I was in life and "what" I could do with all that I had learned and been through at that point.
- Understanding the power of now, meant understanding that only I could determine "when" I wanted to be better and how!

"Life becomes easier when you learn to accept the apology that you never got."
~Robert Brault~

Prayer:

~Serenity Prayer~
God grant me the Serenity to accept the things that I cannot change, the Courage to change the things I can and the Wisdom to know the difference.

Amen!

Chapter Six

Traumas, Triggers and Anger

Psalm 91:4-6

"He will cover you with his pinions, and under his wings you will find refuge; his faithfulness is a shield and buckler. You will not fear the terror of the night, nor the arrow that flies by day, nor the pestilence that stalks in darkness, nor the destruction that wastes at noonday."

"None of us get to wear a mask, all the time." The words spoken in a message from the first lady of the church I attended. Those words resonated with me to my core. At that point, the journey to my wholeness had begun. "None of us get to wear a mask ALL of the time!" *Good Mourning Nude* is what God was birthing out of me and what he was asking from me. I had to face all that was inside which was now spilling over to the outside. This wasn't the first time my insides came spilling out. For so many years, I masked it. My clothing, career, seemingly picture-perfect family, social media pages, etcetera were fragments of the mask. Meanwhile, I was literally dying on the inside because so much was going on.

When God began to unclothe all that I was holding and hiding from within, I now was **stripped naked** (figuratively). I was **mourning** a life that God was calling me to leave behind. Part of the new birth of destiny was also facing the afterbirth. My placenta of trauma held many uncultivated issues inside. I had to acknowledge and recognize my pain in order to identify my trauma. Those decades of family issues shaped my former thought process. I had to confront family secrets, dysfunctions, generational despondency, abuse, neglect, and spiritual ignorance. The time had come for the healing to begin and the brokenness to be addressed. Sure, I was entitled to feel some way; after all I had gone through. However, I was not allowed to unpack and settle in that place of hopelessness and disappointment. The journey was about healing from the inside of my past.

I had been carrying around this unhealthy placenta sack. It had to come out. God was opening my eyes through my own trauma, triggers and anger. It was about absolute healing. That healing was going to stick and stay!

It wasn't an easy process. There were days that were easier than others. To really address pain, can be agonizing. I soon came to realize why so many refused to or couldn't face doing the work. It was too painful, heavy, exhausting, and emotional. To really recall or relive trauma can be traumatic in itself. People on the outside often ask a very harsh and judgmental question, "What's wrong with him/her?" versus "What happened to him/her?" I had to ask myself that question too. For years, I too walked around in self-judgment asking, "what's wrong?" instead of asking myself, "what happened?" I realized that there were levels of this healing. Being cognizant and observing things that happened from childhood to my present moment was a big part.

Level 1 ~ Facing Trauma

I remember sitting in therapy sessions, discussing events that had taken place in my life. Over the years, I shared about failed relationships, insecurities and brokenness. Every time I retold the events of my life, it resulted in me crying. I'd reach for the nearest tissue box. I hurriedly discarded the tears from my face. The session would end shortly thereafter. Generally, we would have only cracked the surface of my pain. I would leave feeling a minimal release. Sometimes, I would sit for a moment in my car in the parking lot and reflect. The reflection wouldn't last long. I needed to drive and focus on where my next destination was from that point. I also didn't want to wear the pain on my face or posture. I had to shut it off and put my mask on until my next therapy session. At that point, we could possibly revisit where we had previously left off.

Perhaps I didn't always know how to address the things that I was dealing with or articulate my feelings. I did what brokenness commands us to do. I stuffed it deep down inside of me. Life is like that for so many. Some sort of trauma happens and maybe we chose not to deal with it. Perhaps we tried, but what took place was so painful and humiliating that we place it on the shelf. We label it as "Maybe I deserved it. Maybe they didn't mean to hurt me. Hurting people hurt people. I don't want to get anyone in trouble. This will take too long to address. I don't want he/she/them to be upset with me. I really need this job to pay my bills" and so on.

There all kinds of reasons we chose to stuff trauma inside and keep it moving. We keep moving until something happens. If we are not truly healed, we can be snatched back into pain. This can be triggered by something on television. It can happen when we hear something on the radio, or someone says something that reminds us. There are times someone does something that takes us back to that traumatic moment or event. A lot of my trauma laid dormant within me for decades. I wasn't even in a place of awareness, but rather a place of re-traumatizing.

Once we acknowledge trauma, it's very easy to see the effects. On the external, it manifests in what we say, and do, or how we act. Yet, we can be confused by the circumstances that caused the trauma. How? Why? What? When we deepen our attention to the cracks of trauma, the light shines through. We can see it. It is in that moment that we decide if we want to deal with it. When we don't process trauma, we become bound to shame and blame. We start to isolate in order to navigate through the pain.

Isolation can be unhealthy and more damaging. Being left alone with the flood of tormenting thoughts and situations can be risky. I plugged into prayer, bible study and talk therapy. I began researching the effects of trauma. I linked up with support groups that were specific to my trauma. This meant I could surround myself with a loving community. They not only understood but cared about my wellbeing and healing path. I scheduled time for self-care, whether it was taking in a movie by myself, getting a foot massage or my nails painted. There were times I would just sit at the top of the walking trail by Loyola University. I'd stare out into the city of Los Angeles. Sometimes, I would sit in my car, close my eyes, and focus on the audio happening outside my car window.

Part of facing my trauma was becoming aware of it. Acknowledging all the horrible and unfortunate things that happened to me were important too. I wrote each trauma down and I walked through each one. How did the trauma affect me socially, emotionally, physically, and psychologically? Did it stunt my growth in some areas? Once I acknowledged the offense and the associated pain, it was like a fork in the middle of the road. I had to uproot it and not just move past or around it. It meant sometimes I had to sit in that pain for a moment to truly feel it, learn from it, and be healed from it. This was not an overnight success or process. I soon realized that this would be a life-long journey. Daily, I had to choose whether or not I wanted to keep my healing.

Level II ~ Trigger Traps

In the beginning I didn't realize the level of trauma and turmoil. God had to create a level of awareness. He wanted to bring me to a place where I would have the desire to address the trauma. I started asking God to show me and heal me in the areas that were hindering my growth. I also petitioned Him to show me where the triggers were. One of the first things I became aware of was the trigger of disrespect. I had tolerated foolishness and disrespect for far too long. I ended up marrying that trigger. Anytime in my life I felt disrespected or disregarded I would either shut down or voice my disapproval. What purpose did that serve? If I wasn't dealing with the root cause of disrespect.

The next trigger I addressed was loyalty and trust. I was everyone's secret keeper. More times than not, I found that my secrets weren't being held in the same regard. It was probably more traumatic feeling like I couldn't trust anyone. The trigger of being and feeling alone. I swear I really had to walk through this one. I am sure that I have failed people in relationships. I have left individuals feeling void of my care or concern. I struggled with this the most. I believe God was saying, "all you ever have and ever need is in me." I heard a funny story that reminded me of how I felt at times. It was about a little boy who wanted to sleep with his parents during a thunderstorm. The little boy kept asking, "Dad, can I please come and sleep with you and mommy?" The father would lovingly but sternly reply, "No, son, God is with you and he is laying beside you." After the third or fourth time asking and the father lovingly but sternly responding, "No. son. God is with you and he is laying beside you." The little boy replied, "I know that God is with me and laying beside me, but I want to be next to some skin!"

How often do people feel as though they walk through problems and circumstances alone? I put my trust in God and relied on him for my strength. He always let me know that I was not alone. He would use old friends calling out of the blue to check on me. Messages on highway billboards would capture my attention. The answer to my question from my prayer time would always be revealed. A window or door of opportunity always presented itself. God made sure I was not alone, even in times that I felt that way.

These moments of trigger traps can be brought on by pain and disappointments. We get stuck in pause and rewind instead of stop and eject. I did not want to be stuck on pause and continuing to rewind. I wanted out and I wanted to learn how to deal with triggers. I had to address the trauma and stop the disrespect. I also had to continue to be loyal, build trust relationships and nurture the ones I had.

Level III- Agony of Anger

I survived an abusive marriage. Fed up with the pain of disrespect of how I was feeling, invited anger. I was in constant turmoil and I could not understand why. I went from pity to party to party to pity. I was confused. How did I end up in this bad? As I began to reach out for help, I was able to connect with resilient women. This group was aware of their trauma. They were facing them one step at a time. I had reached a point where I had to face my reality. With that reality came the acknowledgment of fear, pain, and brokenness. There was an awareness awakening inside of me. Suddenly, I began a deeper journey with God to truly do the work. This was necessary for me to become whole and address my anger. Journeying the path to becoming whole was not only just work, it meant that I had to go back and face the haunted house. This house was my past and that past ran as far back as I could remember.

The work was an ongoing process. Therefore, my therapy was running much longer than 40-50 minutes. It was more than once to twice a month, on a comfy couch. In these sessions, I would be pouring my all out to an unbiased stranger. I had to join forces with the strongest and baddest life coach/counselor/friend ever. That coach was God. I can honestly say, God allowed me to walk through the angry phase of my trauma. I believe he was truly allowing me to feel every bit of my healing journey. How can you talk about something that you have never gone or lived through?!

Over time, I realized that I traumatized myself in some ways. It was a mistake, relying only on my faith to change my marriage, husband, and circumstances. In doing this I misinterpreted pain as love, anger as a way of showing that one cared. I didn't realize God would never want me or my children to be subjected to abuse or ruled by anyone.

I hated having my family ripped apart and publicly humiliated. Eventually, the shame awakened my boiling anger of injustice and despair. There were many times that I would be so inwardly upset about the dysfunction and destruction. I would literally be shouting and crying to God. Hitting the car steering wheel out of frustration and anger I'd question, "Why won't you do anything, God? Do you see what's going on? My children and I are facing homelessness. Are you really going to allow them to tell those lies?" I was livid and reliving trauma every day. My situation and circumstances had power and control over my emotions. Through the agony of anger, I realized that the attacks on me and my family's life was about distracting and rerouting me from the purpose and journey of healing. Anger was trying to stifle my birthing and creativity. It wanted to hinder what had already been assigned to my life, before I was even formed in my mother's womb!

I had to learn to shut out all outside noises to hear the inner voice of my spirit calling fervently, peacefully, and quietly. The negative thoughts replaying in my mind were causing me to listen. It was a negative voice of anger. If we get caught up listening to the negative, we start seeing negativity. Then we experience a limited worldview of our purpose. I believe there is purpose in one's pain. That pain can be turned into power. I developed righteous indignation for the truth to prevail. Those in bondage and captivity to trauma would be set free. They can then choose the journey to wholeness and healing.

My fear of facing the trauma and being triggered and living in the agony of anger was trying to succumb me. It threatened to keep me trapped inside an infant state of mind. We all have access to the same emotions. We go through cycles of fear, abandonment, desiring to be loved and to love. We have to develop and use our strength and resilience. This allows us to push past and push through to healing and wholeness. We can manage and balance our perspective, to grow and stay in the cycle of change.

How we handle and manage change is a big focus to our awareness of the trauma, triggers and anger. Change can be challenging. In most cases, change is good and necessary. Facing fears, defeating odds and overcoming trauma can transform into motivation, determination, inspiration and elevation. This is not only your own life, but also impacting lives around you! You must know who you are, where you have been and where you are headed. This is vital to walk the guided path of your destiny and purpose. In closing, I will share what I heard while writing this chapter, "Pain didn't break you, it changed you. It sparked a fire inside of you to desire to be a part of change and to be a part of the nation's healing."

Prayer:

I pray this day and every day that we would live our best lives NOW! I pray for mental clarity in speech, actions and deeds. I ask for the continued desire, power, energy and strength to make healthy choices. I pray for wisdom and discernment of what we put into our minds by way of radio, television, social media, daily news and by what we speak over ourselves. May we learn to block negative energy that seeks to drain and destroy us. May we develop the skills to know better and do better in our personal, financial, business, family, political, health and relationship decision-making. May we be set free from all bondages that are there to paralyze, stifle our growth and clear the resistance to change. In the Heavenly Fathers name I pray and ask all these things.

Amen!

Part 3

CALL OF DUTY

JEREMIAH 29:11-13

"For I know the plans I have for you, declares the Lord, plans for welfare and not for evil, to give you a future and a hope. Then you will call upon me and come and pray to me, and I will hear you. You will seek me and find me, when you seek me with all your heart."

Chapter Seven

UNMUTED
When her silence was broken

Ephesians 5:11 (ESV)

"Take no part in the unfruitful works of darkness, but instead expose them."

When her silence was broken,
she had nowhere to run.

When her silence was broken,
her journey had just begun.

When her silence was broken,
she had many needs.

But that silence being broken,
brought her crashing to her knees.

Though her silence had been broken,
she had no clue what to do.

When that silence was broken,
she was void of help and unable to
see her way through.

When her silence was broken,
judgment, slander and fear came.

When her silence was broken,
all she felt was humiliation and shame.

When her silence was broken,
she knew that she had to survive.

When her silence was broken,
she couldn't see the other side.

The other side to hope,
freedom and a voice to save
her children cried deep inside.

When her silence was broken,

she reached out and found.

*Silence was the very thing that
kept her bound.*

*Silence was chained to darkness
and darkness chained to death.*

*When her silence was broken,
she had to walk away never turning back,
for she had nothing left.*

*When her silence was broken,
the resources and help were there.*

*Silence being broken, allowed her to reach,
grab and her journey became clear.*

*She prayed, she fasted and the answers
came from God above.*

*Her silence being broken brought a myriad
of support with God's heart and love.*

*Many were her advocates and
many were angels in flesh.*

*These great pioneers and warriors,
stood with her through many great
battles and test.*

*When her silence was broken,
she knew the road would be lonely
and sometimes distant.*

By her silence being broken,

she endured great pain and
intense resistance.

When her silence was broken,
she realized there were others
waiting on her story.

By her silence being broken,
it would save many and
bring God glory.

Many nights she lay awake and pray.
Many days she sent up an S.O.S.
for God to save the day.

When her silence was broken,
it was her faith and hope that
opened many doors.

Her faith and her prayers gave her
strength to face each day.

When her silence was broken,
she had visions of women and
children trapped in despair.

By her silence being broken,
it opened many eyes, hearts and
minds for those that were not aware.

When her silence was broken,
she stood not only for her
generations past.

By her silence being broken,

at last a nation's darkness
was unmasked.

Her silence being broken,
allowed her to see the mantle
she had to carry.

When her silence was broken,
defeat and depression, she had to bury.

When her silence was broken,
she realized healing was along the path.

When her silence was broken,
she learned to navigate through
the aftermath.

When her silence was broken,
she reached to God as her ultimate source.

When silence was broken,
the angels of whom God sent
were the carrying force.

When her silence was broken,
she walked in her truth and became
empowered by her story.
For all things work together for
our good and can be used for God's glory.

When her silence was broken,
she realized only she could tell her truth.

By her silence being broken.
It was the feet of her faith that
propelled her to move.

When her silence was broken,
all lies, and forces of darkness had to flee.

When her silence was broken.
Her truth became the wind
beneath her wings.

Through her silence being broken.
She was now connected to many
great women who shared the same.

The Sojourn of truth and the
history behind their names.

Giving homage to many who
fought the battle before her.

When her silence was broken,
those women of truth became
powerful sorrors.

Now that her silence had been broken,
she could not let generations past down.

For the steps taken and the tears they cried,
was a paved road of celebrated resilience.
and significant stride.

When her silence was broken,
freedom rang for many women and children.

But what about the ones who had been
silenced and put to death.

Those with hearts cracked

and words unspoken.

When her silence was broken,
she heard "stand tall, hold your
head up high."

This was a way for society,
justice and all nations to see
the God inside.

Putting on the full armor of God,
broke barriers and sent bombs
into the enemy's camp.

By her silence being broken,
she became strong in God's mighty power.

The Lion of the Tribe of Judah,
captured the enemy and brought
him to his own devour.

With the belt of truth, the breastplate
of righteousness, the feet of peace,
the shield of faith, the sword of God's
word and the helmet of salvation.
Her silence was finally broken,
and God granted her family a
generational restoration.

When her silence was broken!

~*Maury Danielle*~

Steps to Breaking the Silence

(Steps to make, direction to take)

- **Accept what you can't change and pray for the courage to change the things that you can:**
    o Take one day at a time, putting one foot in front of the other.
    o Do the best with what you have in front of you with what you have access to.
    o When you put movement to your feet, the path and doors will open.

- **Journal your thoughts, incidents, actions, and progress:**
    o Keep them in a safe place (safety deposit box, storage, electronic file, etc.).
    o Create a private email account that only you know about and have access to. With this account store all documents, photos, and important information electronically. Create an email storage hub.
    o Write emails and letters to yourself and to significant others that can one day be shared if and when the time is appropriate.

- **Tell a trusted Godly counsel and/or source:**
    o Use wisdom when sharing and use discernment on who to share with.
    o Seek answers and directions through biblical scripture and stories.

o Take inventory of your support system. Navigating where you are in your journey of healing is important when assessing your needs.

- **Find support groups in your area or nearby that accommodate your situation:**
  o Grievance counseling or support groups.
  o Domestic violence counseling or support groups.
  o Substance and alcohol abuse counseling or support groups.
  o Adolescent support groups.
  o Community support groups.

- **Get rest:**
  o You will have high and low moments. Take those needed breaks for your mental wellness and physical health.
  o Remember there is a process to process.
  o Self-care is needed care. Ex: take naps, go for a drive, and go to bed early, vacation, quick getaway.
  o Stay calm.

- **Ask for help. Remember that darkness and despair thrive in silence:**
  o Calling 211 from your cell phone or landline to inquire about specific resources.
  o Your local courthouse may have a self-help center that can assist with preparing documents, give legal advice or have access or information for specific resources that you may need.

o Remember there is no such thing as a stupid question.
o Be resourceful. Research resources and create resources.

- **Do your research on specific matters:**
  o Your local library gives access to books, computers, internet, and publications.
  o Create a YouTube account where you can bookmark and store various videos, tutorials, empowerment messages and teachings relating to the subject matter.
  o If there is something you don't know don't be afraid to ask.

- **Develop a plan:**
  o Action plan.
  o Safety plan.
  o Mental and Physical health plan.
  o Have faith but remember faith without works is void of hope.

"Even the things that look broken beyond repair have a chance at being whole again. It just depends how much you want to rebuild it."

~ Natasha Preston, Broken Silence

Prayer:

Loving and caring, Heavenly Father. I come to you now asking for your guidance and your strength to break the silence. God, I know that silence is chained to darkness. Thoughts of hopelessness, shame and humiliation are not of you. Take captive, thoughts of fear, worry and doubt and allow the truth to be found. Lord, help me strategize and develop a plan for safety and action. Help me to see what areas I need help in. In getting help, I will be able to share my story. It will help others come out of silence and darkness. Be my strong tower. You are my rescue and defense. I send up a supernatural S.O.S flare that you may hear my prayers, see my heart and move on my behalf. Thank you for the little, and the big steps and for the rest along the way. I'm putting actions to my faith and trust in you.

Amen!

Chapter Eight

Good Mourning Nude
(Out of the Fog)

Matthew 5:3-12 (NLT)

"God blesses those who are poor and realize their need for him, for the Kingdom of Heaven is theirs. **God blesses those who mourn, for they will be comforted.** *God blesses those who are humble, for they will inherit the whole earth. God blesses those who hunger and thirst for justice, for they will be satisfied. God blesses those who are merciful, for they will be shown mercy. God blesses those whose hearts are pure, for they will see God. God blesses those who work for peace, for they will be called the children of God. God blesses those who are persecuted for doing right, for the Kingdom of Heaven is theirs. "God blesses you when people mock you and persecute you and lie about you and say all sorts of evil things against you because you are my followers. Be happy about it! Be very glad! For a great reward awaits you in heaven. And remember, the ancient prophets were persecuted in the same way."*

Who knew that there could ever be such beauty in mourning and pain? That was most definitely not my thoughts. For years people would complement my name being "Maury Mourning." I would smile and agree that the name is quite unique and one of a kind. At the same time, I could not help thinking about all of the pain I had lived through, after the changing of my last name. Many trials and tribulations birthed from carrying Mourning as my surname. Since then, I have been catapulted into a divinely appointed shift. This shift, alignment or however you would reference it, permitted boundless growth and strength. It was more far-reaching than I ever imagined it could or would have been.

This journey is one to be proud of because what did not kill me, made me stronger, wiser, better and fearless. I continue to be optimistic about what the future holds for the lives of me and my children. My faith exceeds my earthly expectations. My relationship with my Heavenly Father, gracefully ruins me every day. This is because the Lord continues to perfect his good work in me. My life intentions and purpose have become defined and clear. I realized that if you have never gone through something life changing or altering, how can you relate to others. How do you truly speak to the need of the people if you can't relate?

We all have experienced loss at some point in time in our lives. Those who grieve, and mourn, can grieve because of the death of a loved one. It can be because of a loss of a career or opportunity, friendship, a home, or a sentimental keepsake. A car, a special ring or that favorite baseball cap that your dad gave to you when he was alive are catalyst for grief. Perhaps you grieve the loss of hugs and kisses from your late grandparents. Maybe you mourn a certain lifestyle that you no longer seem privy to. Many mourn the loss of their children or a significant other. Some have lost pets. Some have lost money, wealth, dignity and respect, while others have literally lost their minds from a traumatic event. No one can judge or measure someone else's pain and or disappointments.

My grief transposed into depression. It felt as if I was fading into the abyss of hopelessness because of all the shock and trauma that my mind and body had gone through. My mind kicked into overdrive and a protective state. I started experiencing a lot of brain fog; a state of mental confusion, detachment, and forgetfulness. It can be a cognitive deficit discovered in depression and domestic violence. The unrecognized grief or denial of such, can turn into depression. Depression undiagnosed, and untreated can lead to a spiritual, emotional, mental and sometimes physical death!

Many times, I have thought about the late and great, Whitney Houston and her beloved daughter, Bobby Kristina. I just remember in 2015 around the time Bobby Kristina passed, I was battling a very dark and deep depression. My heart was heavy for what Bobbi Kristina Brown must have been going through the years after her mother's death. The grief behind that great loss seemed to have emerged her into depression. It appeared she'd lost her hope and will to live. It was very sad and traumatic circumstances for the Houston and Brown family to have lived through. Grief and depression are very complicated and sometimes hard to put into words, often hard to detect right away or even explain to someone how you feel.

A person's actions and behaviors may appear strange, aloof or distant to someone who is only looking at the exterior facts. Sometimes people attempt to mask the internal torment going on. When a person is grieving and dealing with depression, their reactions, actions and emotions can be inconstant, intense and sometimes irrational. One can feel like they are losing their mind. I remember feeling like I was losing my mind during various times of my depression. It felt like I was grasping at straws, trying to keep everything in me and around me from crumbling. Hindsight, my depression lasted as long as it did partially due to my prolonged grief. There were times I was battling grief while being afraid to confront it. It seemed I was in shock and denial for a good amount of time. That shock and denial kept me from addressing grief and depression. Back then when I was suffering through and with so much, I couldn't see myself on the other side. I couldn't imagine the fog lifting. I couldn't even imagine being happy because I didn't see myself ever escaping my circumstances.

No matter what our traumatic experiences and circumstances may be, grief does not last forever. However, it can be prolonged, and it certainly is a process. Depending on the individual, their level of grief and how it is addressed, time cannot be determined or measured. However, if we acknowledge our feelings, we can work through the process of becoming healed and whole. When we try to deny our reactions to grief, battling through depression alone, we can become stagnant. This disposition does not serve one's well-being. I say that with all confidence and conviction. I know what that stagnant place feels like. My stagnation was not always a choice. There were times I looked back. I saw where pride and denial of my reality stifled my progression towards healing.

Safety, strength, love, stability, trust, loyalty, and having control over my life were some major characteristics of who I was. It was also how my family, friends, and others had known me to be. With denial and shock being the sister-cousin as so closely related to the daughter-aunt of grief and depression, I was just trying to hold it all together. I didn't want to believe that the horrific details and things that were happening to me and my family were really taken place. Not to "Maury", no, no, no, no, no. Maury did not marry too quickly. Maury did not lose her close friend to stage-four breast and brain cancer. Maury did not move all the way to California from Texas to be isolated from friends and family. Maury did not go from making money of her own to now borrowing money from others and receiving help from friends and family. Maury was not involved in a very toxic and abusive relationship. What do you mean she can't leave or get out of it? Did she really not get to say goodbye to her childhood best friends before they suddenly died?

I was my own worst critic, judge and jury. I was the committee of said folks who were looking down upon me with judgment. I was too proud for the longest time to tell anyone what I was dealing with behind closed doors. I didn't want to expose who I believed was the love or my life, my soulmate, my God-given partner. I believed that I could love him through his pain. The pain that caused him to act and behave in the manors of which he did time and time and time again.

I have always been a "FIXER." The emotional and verbal abuse from my spouse came as a real curveball—with speed. I was not prepared for my life to take an unexpected and unsolicited violent turn. It kept spinning until I landed on my knees and eventually on my face. I begged God to release me from the very thing I had previously asked him to release me too! My own pride prevented me from seeing the truth about my circumstances. The truth is, deep down inside I lived with a lot of false narratives. One narrative was that folks were so concerned about what I was doing. Another narrative was that they had a right to judge me or be disappointed in my life. That was all me.

I started grieving my marriage while I was in it. I mourned the disappointment of things not being what I thought and believed marriage to be. It just broke me down. I wanted my marriage to work. I really loved my husband for who I thought that he was and could be as a husband, father and friend. I gripped tightly to all the good times, laughter, travel and the success that came and went intermittently. I became somewhat co-dependent in that relationship. I thought it could provide healing, wholeness, safety, security, trust, and loyalty. Those were all the things that I always wanted. Praying, fasting and clinging to God's word is what got me through some of the roughest patches of my life. I was divinely connected continuously with individuals that seemed to be angels in the flesh. It was as if they were sent for spiritual and emotional guidance. They were planted there to get me from the place where I was. I was walking through the fog instead of the fog subjectively staring me in my face. My grief was looking at the fog approaching. My depression was standing in the fog unable to see my way through.

The fog began to lift when I started doing the work towards changing my circumstances. The same was true when I started changing my mindset. Change meant, taking a hard look at myself. Also, digging deep down into my soul, looking at the root cause of many areas of my life. I saw my insecurities, resentments, anger, fears, rejections, and disappointments. I started plugging into the resources that were afforded to me. I sought counseling that addressed the abuse. I also dealt with the trauma that I was suffering through. Then I educated myself on the subjects matters that I was dealing with. Like a big elephant in the room, I began to eat one piece at a time. As I did this, my focus became clearer. I went from standing in the fog to seeing through the fog, to the fog lifting, one layer at a time. Meanwhile, I kept walking towards light and hope.

I know it was God that pulled me out and through a very toxic and debilitating circumstance. Where would I be, if it had not been for the grace, mercy, and power of God? I listened to God's word even when I didn't feel like it. Going through counseling, attending support groups were helpful. Pulling strength from other women around me helped me to be present.

Researching, educating and uncovering the truth about my circumstances aided in my recovery. I changed my environment, thus changing my circle of people and friends, thoughts and mindset. I no longer wanted to attract or be attracted to those things that reminded me of who I used to be. I was once unsure of who I was. Those things that would keep me in the vicious cycle of repeat, replay, and rewind. The Girl that was interrupted and rebirthed into a woman of *Good Mourning Nude*. I have overcome several obstacles. I suffered a lot of pain and healed from many scars. Many spiritual operations were endured. Ultimately, I tried on many glasses to fit the right pair of lenses. I've gone from crawling to walking. Then I went from flapping to flying, transforming to become all that I am today. I realized that none of this would have been possible if I wasn't able to bare my naked truth. The good truth of mourning. The losses were actually victories in the end.

I found some alarming truths. A significant amount of the 21st century suicides is due to mental illness of depression. The rate is unbelievably high. Unlike the thoughts that come into our minds, we are not alone. I believe that everyone has felt or gone through a level of depression or grief. Please know, there is a myriad of hope and help available. Reach out to a trusted source. Seek help today (see additional resources in the back of this book). There is a life worth living awaiting you!

The fog was progressively lifted through my journey. This allowed me to see the potency and power of my untamed prophetic "Life turned upside down" dream. This dream would flash flood my mind over the years. I would ask God to interpret, reveal or uncover the fullness of this dream. I now count it all as joy. Through this process, I have learned that I can turn my pain into power. It can be someone's hope, rescue, safety, awareness, comfort and peace. My truth is reliant upon me baring the naked truth of my pain. My pain is not to be minimized at all. It is to be used for God's good works and glory.

My pain has purpose. The intentions were created to destroy a generational target placed on my family. My mourning losses had to be exposed to bring light to darkness, to bring hope to despair. It also brings about a safe landing and a life well lived in my children. I had to make a choice, exposing the history of the enemy of lies. The secrets and abuse in my family and my marriage had to be revealed. The old foundation had to be dug up. The ground had to be tilled, so we could lay a new foundation. It had to be strong for my children and my children's children to firmly stand upon it.

You have to shut out all outside noise to hear the inner voice of your spirit calling fervently, yet quietly. If we get caught up listening to the negativity, we start seeing negativity. We experience a limited worldview of our calling. We must be strong and resilient enough to push past and through to success. I once heard Jay Z say, "I would rather live enormous than to die dormant."

You have to manage and balance your perspective. It will help you grow and stay in the cycle of change. How we handle and manage change effects our awareness. Change can be challenging. In most cases, change is good and necessary. Facing fears, defeating odds of success calls for one to truly evaluate and invest in self. You have to know who you are and where you are in order to walk the guided path of your destiny and purpose. You have to choose a lighted path. Stumbling around in darkness only harnesses your fears and keeps you stagnant. Motivation, determination, inspiration, and elevation are all keys to empower to change.

Prayer:

Father God, we thank you for lifting the layers of fog. We thank you for keeping us protected and guarded from harmful thoughts and actions. We believe that you are the way, the light and the truth to our healing and wholeness. We ask that you continue to place individuals, resources, support group communities and spiritual guidance in our path that would allow us to reach a safe landing place. We thank you that we grow through what we go through and that we do not remain stagnant. Continue to cover our minds and thoughts in hope, peace and love. Continue to give us the courage to pull down strongholds and destroy generational imprecations and help us not to repeat historical dysfunctions from past generations. Help us to walk in your truth and to not be ashamed of our story. For there is power in testimony and your perfect love cast out fear! In your holy and precious name.

Amen!

Chapter Nine

From Pit to Power - Olympus Mandate
(Heavens Commissioning)

John 20:21

Jesus said to them again, "Peace be with you. As the Father has sent me, even so I am sending you."

A New Lease on Life

1 Corinthians 2:9-16: ***What no eye has seen, what no ear has heard, and what no human mind has conceived*** *the things God has prepared for those who love him these are the things God has revealed to us by his Spirit. The Spirit searches all things, even the deep things of God. For who knows a person's thoughts except their own spirit within them? In the same way no one knows the thoughts of God except the Spirit of God. What we have received is not the spirit of the world, but the Spirit who is from God, so that we may understand what God has freely given us. This is what we speak, not in words taught us by human wisdom but in words taught by the Spirit, explaining spiritual realities with Spirit-taught words. The person without the Spirit does not accept the things that come from the Spirit of God but considers them foolishness and cannot understand them because they are discerned only through the Spirit. The person with the Spirit makes judgments about all things, but such a person is not subject to merely human judgments, for,* ***who has known the mind of the Lord so as to instruct him?*** *But we have the mind of Christ.*

Years ago, shortly after relocating to California, I had a dream that still resonates. This dream foretold and confirmed this Good Mourning Nude appeal to my heart. I believe it was an Olympus Mandate to write this book. The process of this project coming to life influenced my overall journey to wholeness. I remember a man of God being in that dream   He kept commending me on how I was dealing with my husband and my marriage. When I woke up from that dream, I wrote everything down as my spirit was leading me to recall the message. I didn't want to forget the greatest message of all, "Olympus Mandate." When I looked up the word Olympus, I found this powerful meaning, "A poetic word for heaven."

I have exerted so much energy in my life to the wrong people and situations. Moving from "Pit to Power" is about having the right perspectives in my life. Moving forward in true healing and power to impact lives for healthy and lasting change. It speaks to me being the best version of myself possible. I can walk alongside those that desire to do the work and be well. I am growing confidently into who I am every day. Writing this book has been a source of healing. I am pleased with who I am becoming and the truth of who I am. Learning to shut out all the outside noise to hear has cultivated me. There is now an inner voice of my spirit calling me. It beckons me to go deeper, fervently, and quietly out of fear of the unknown.

Your fears will always try to paralyze and keep you trapped inside a limited mindset and environment. In God, I am strong. I am also resilient enough to push through to the place where God is calling me. It came through my faith and intimate time with God. Through prayer and fasting, I sought healing and wholeness. It fulfilled my desire to be well and free of debilitating circumstances. You are confirmation of God calling you out of darkness into his guided light.

This new lease on life dream was yet another catalyst involving change. Not only did it involve change, it was a hallmark of truth. It was preparing me for the journey that I had been on with God. Despite what I have been through and survived to, God had a plan. He sent what I like to call the S.O.S.

community. This encompassed messengers in my dreams to give me hope and confirmation. I needed to know that I was on the right path. All the pieces of the puzzle were now coming together. They were preparing to form a big picture which was my assignment and my heavenly mandate. Through this mandate, lives would be changed. My life would personally and dramatically be transformed. I had renewed hope that all things were going to work together for my good. I was on target with the assignment of writing a book. Later, I would discover not just one book, but several books. Was I now ready to level up and allow the wings that God had given to me to take flight? Was I ready to go to a place of true vulnerability, transparency and ability to be used by God? The answer was and is, yes. The late Dr. Myles Munroe often said, "We must die empty." I've wasted a lot of time waiting for love, the right people, opportunities to just show up. I wasted time waiting for things to fall in line.

One day, I was driving down the 405 freeway. I was listening to Bishop TD Jakes on YouTube. He said something in his message that was so profound. I mean, it totally shook my inner core and completely registered with me. He said, "Stop worrying about the destination and just enjoy the journey." Man, that was major for me. I had spent previous years trying to figure things out. I was resisting the journey. Often, the resistance included my dreams. Why did God send me to California? I moved away from family and friends, a real support system.

For all intents and purposes, they could help me through the biggest challenges of my life.

Why had God chosen this time to expose the negative truths about my marriage? Why go through a divorce in California, where I had no family, no familiar support system? Why did I have to endure one of the most disappointing hardships and set-backs ever? Trying to figure out why things were happening the way that they were. At least four years, but really like eight to nine years had gone by. More importantly, at the time that I heard that message by T.D. Jakes.

At least seven years had gone by since I had that tripped out dream. The one at my girlfriend's home, "Life turned upside down" in 2009. Now, hitting the fast forward button to the pass-ing of some close and special friends. It just felt like my world had gone through some very catastrophic storms and it had. My life had already been abnormal. It felt very much like things kept kicking up into high gear. I had been in a tailspin.

As I was driving down the freeway that day I heard Bishop Jakes say, "Stop worrying about the destination and just enjoy the journey." It was confirmation to what I felt like inside weeks prior to hearing what Bishop Jakes said. I felt like I had been in the middle of somewhere. I felt emotionally, physi-cally, and spiritually drained and stuck. I felt like I didn't belong anywhere. I was not supposed to be in Texas where I previously called home. I didn't belong in the Midwest where I was raised, nor in the North where my parents were from. I felt very stuck in California. It wasn't just due to the abusive marriage. The child we had together could not be taken out of California state jurisdiction. I could also feel the shift of a huge transition in my life happening. I was no longer the same person I was, 1, 2, 5 or even 10-years prior. I had literally walked out my freedom, my hope, my healing, my faith and now my families charted and predestined course of generational freedom.

In the early part of 2016, my depression started to emerge. The brain fog was being lifted. The pressure of life and my circumstances started to release. I felt as though I could at least breathe metaphorically. However, I remember feeling like I just didn't belong anywhere. My circumstances were screaming for me to leave California. My heart and mind were not in any of the places that I had lived before. Several people inquired if I was going to move back to Texas. They wanted to know because I was seemingly having a tough time in California. I couldn't really describe it after a while. I loved California and one point hated California. When one of my friends asked me, "Do you think you would go back to Texas?" I answered as honest as my heart and mind had felt for a while. "I don't know, I feel like I don't belong anywhere. It's like I'm in the middle of nowhere. I'm somewhere I can't describe!" That's exactly how I had been feeling for months. I felt the release of the weight of depression emerging from me. I was starting to take it one step at a time towards rebuilding and regaining control of my life. It was going to be a long journey. Things had been such a mess for so long. It felt like there was a huge amount of damage control to be done. I didn't know where to start. There was a lot of work ahead of me. I was still in a very toxic and abusive marriage at the time. Just as Bishop Jakes had said, "Enjoy the journey." Thankfully, I desired to nurture my relationship with God through prayer, meditation, reading my daily devotional and listening to good spiritually sound teachings. These things were the key to regaining my strength and power. They were key to emotional, psychological and in a major way physical health.

When your mind and emotions are in a healthy place it gives energy to your body and vice versa. Physical exercise helps to improve your mood as it increases the production of serotonin. Exercise aids as a natural antidepressant by increasing serotonin levels in your brain. The more I exercised and worked on feeling better, the stronger I was becoming. I started opening up more about the things that I was going through. Talking about things certainly seemed to help.

Moving from pit to power! I accepted the things that had taken place over the course of my life and the truth about my marriage. I started noticing the stages of what I was going through. I was grieving all the losses in my life. Step by step, God began to dig deeper into my soul and showed me what needed to be addressed. He showed me where the roots were coming from. My eyes were open to how dark and deep the damage was. I had to make a choice whether to allow my past disappointments and pain to ferment into further chaos. The turmoil could ultimately destroy me and my children's life. I had to decide if I was going to take the good with the bad. Was I going to take the bitter with the sweet? Would I elect to make a new song? I would develop a new rhythm with the melodies of my heart and soul. As God dug deeper, it propelled me forward to climb out of the pit of hopelessness. I literally clung to the spiritual truths and words of hope. They held the framework to the faith that had sustained me throughout the years.

I'll never forget the words that Pastor Bayless Conley, my former pastor spoke over me. During an event at Cottonwood Church in Los Alamitos, CA he said, "No matter how long it takes, you and your children will receive a great reward." I didn't have a full understanding of what he meant. However, it was words of hope in very challenging times in my life. Over the years, I would continue to hear his voice and that very statement. It was as if I was standing in front of him all over again. Those words that Pastor Conley had spoken over me were from God. A word of hope and promise of a renewed and expected day. I can say that I am standing in that reward today. The promises of God and his word continue to reward me and my family daily as I seek His will for my life.

A part of moving from surviving to thriving is that you have to manage and balance your perspective. This aids in growth and helps us stay in the cycle of change. We should not resist the change. It is inevitable in our lives in powering us to move forward. We are moving toward new dimensions and levels. How we manage change is a big focus to our awareness. It can be challenging. In most phases of our lives, it's necessary. There is a heavenly mandate on your life that calls you to rise above, be greater, stronger, wiser and be true to you. Know thy self, love yourself, trust the process and see the process of growth, healing and God's perfect love for you!

"You can either stay distracted by your past or you can stay focused on your future!"

~ author unknown

Prayer:

Heavenly Father. Thank you for this book, this journey, this message of hope. Thank you for protecting my soul and for covering my mind. Thank you that in the darkness, your light still shines through. Let your cracked vessels know that your light will always shine through and be that radiant light of hope, strength and healing. Thank you for the heavenly mandate that you have on our lives. You never leave us nor forsake us. Thank you for impacting lives around the world so that your people will come together and shine like a high-quality diamond. In Christ name we pray.

Amen!

"May the Lord bless you and keep you; may the Lord make his face shine on you and be gracious to you; may the Lord turn his face toward you and grant unto you shalom."

Numbers 6:24-26

PART 4

SURVIVING TO THRIVING

Philippians 3:13-14

"Brethren, I do not regard myself as having laid hold of it yet; but one thing I do: forgetting what lies behind and reaching forward to what lies ahead, I press on toward the goal for the prize of the upward call of God in Christ Jesus.

Postface
From Surviving to Thriving

Now I lay me down to sleep,
I pray to the Lord my soul he keeps.
If I should die before I WAKE,
I pray to the Lord, my soul he Takes!
Many days I have felt unworthy.
I wasn't sure that I could complete my journey.

Many times, I've bumped my head.
Many days, I've cried in bed.
I had sleepless nights and dreadful days.
I besiege the pain to go away.
Bound by generational and self-willed condemnation,
birthed into a society of sinful replications.

Chained by thoughts of unworthiness, isolated by fear.
Feeling the breath of the end so near.
Faith shattered by my spiritual demise.
Handicapped by my own self-pride.
Pity was her name, pain was HIS game.
Covered in self-loathing and walking in shame.

Downward spiraling from disappointment.
Save me, Oh Lord, from the enemy's appointment!
I did not schedule this shift, nor did I prepare for this drift.
Please send your angels soon. Father, I need a lift.
I've changed from begging to pleading.
Yet, these wounds keep bleeding.

My spirit bruised, my heart stabbed many times. I'm reaching
for control. I need a stop, reset or rewind.
Seasons have come and gone, yet, I still remain the same.
Same place, same space
as though I am starring death in the face.
Standing at the edge of the cliff,
wishing my life had just been a myth.

Feeling invisible, then suddenly, boom, switch, click.
There was a heavenly shift.
I heard your whisper releasing my doubts.
The feeling of your angels around and about.
A reprieve had come, and the fog had been lifted.
My spirit felt light and no longer conflicted.
There were no more dark clouds around.
Just healing from the damage from when I was down.

All was well with my soul.
There was a confidence that you were with me.
One step at a time. A new day granted unto thee.
Suddenly I had wings. I began to fly free!
Oh' Lord, how can I ever repay you for what was to be?
You're sculpting, you're molding of a caterpillar born free.

Your purpose, your plan to place my mess in your hands.
Creating something so colorful for the world to see.
Your handy work fashioning something so beautiful
still astonishes me.

You were not created to crawl.
You were meant to fly! Soar on butterfly, soar on and thrive.

Power Scriptures

Psalm 23:5 Before my enemies *"You prepare a table before me in the presence of my enemies. You anoint my head with oil; my cup overflows."*

Proverbs 9:10 Fear of a God is beginning of knowledge *"For the reverence and fear of God are basic to all wisdom. Knowing God results in every other kind of understanding."*

James 5:16 Repentance and Prayer *"Therefore, confess your sins to one another, and pray for one another so that you may be healed. The effective prayer of a righteous man can accomplish much."*

Ephesians 6:18 Prayer/Prayer Language *"With all prayer and petition pray at all times in the Spirit, and with this in view, be on the alert with all perseverance and petition for all the saints."*

Hebrews 4:12 The power of the Word *"God reveals to us the nature and function of the Logos: "For the word [Logos] of God is living and active and sharper than any two-edged sword, and piercing as far as the division of soul and spirit, of both joints and marrow, and able to judge the thoughts and intentions of the heart."*

Proverbs 23:7 Guard your Mind *"Don't associate with evil men; don't long for their favors and gifts. Their kindness is a trick; they want to use you as their pawn. The delicious food they serve will turn sour in your stomach, and you will vomit it and have to take back your words of appreciation for their "kindness."*

Proverbs 10:22 Blessings of the Lord *"The blessing of the Lord, it maketh rich, and he addeth no sorrow with it."*

Philippians 4:19 Supplying Needs *"And my God will meet all your needs according to the riches of his glory in Christ Jesus."*

Isaiah 26:3 Peace *"You will keep in perfect peace those whose minds are steadfast, because they trust in you."*

Hebrews 11:1 Walk by Faith *"Now faith is confidence in what we hope for and assurance about what we do not see."*

2 Corinthians 5:7 Live by Faith *"For we live by faith, not by sight."*

Habakkuk 2:4 Righteous live by Faith *"See, the enemy is puffed up; his desires are not upright, but the righteous person will live by his faithfulness…"*

Galatians 5:16 Walk by the Spirit *"So I say, walk by the Spirit, and you will not gratify the desires of the flesh."*

John 10:10 Know your Enemy *"The thief comes only to steal and kill and destroy; I have come that they may have life and have it to the full."*

Psalm 37:25 Trust *"I was young and now I am old, yet I have never seen the righteous forsaken or their children begging bread."*

Ephesians 6:12 Spiritual Warfare *"For our struggle is not against flesh and blood, but against the rulers, against the authorities, against the powers of this dark world and against the spiritual forces of evil in the heavenly realms."*

Ephesians 6:10:17 The Armor of God *"Finally, be strong in the Lord and in his mighty power. Put on the full armor of God, so that you can take your stand against the devil's schemes. For our struggle is not against flesh and blood, but against the rulers, against the authorities, against the powers of this dark world and against the spiritual forces of evil in the heavenly realms. Therefore, put on the full armor of God, so that when the day of evil comes, you may be able to stand your ground, and after you have done everything, to stand. Stand firm then, with the belt of truth buckled around your waist, with the breastplate of righteousness in place, and with your feet fitted with the readiness that comes from the gospel of peace. In addition to all this, take up the shield of faith, with which you can extinguish all the flaming arrows of the evil one. Take the helmet of salvation and the sword of the Spirit, which is the word of God."*

Hebrews 12:2   Focus on Christ through Faith *"Fixing our eyes on Jesus, the pioneer and perfecter of faith. For the joy set before him he endured the cross, scorning its shame, and sat down at the right hand of the throne of God."*

Galatians 2:20   Faith *"I have been crucified with Christ and I no longer live, but Christ lives in me. The life I now live in the body, I live by faith in the Son of God, who loved me and gave himself for me."*

Habakkuk 2:3   Vision *"For the revelation awaits an appointed time; it speaks of the end and will not prove false. Though it linger, wait for it; it will certainly come and will not delay."*

Ephesians 6:23:24 Peace and Love for Fellow Christians/ Brethren *"Peace to the brothers, and love with faith from God the Father and the Lord Jesus Christ. Grace to all who love our Lord Jesus Christ with an undying love."*

The Names of God

El Shaddai
Lord God Almighty

El Elyon
The Most-High God

Adonai
Lord, Master

Yahweh
Lord, Jehovah

Jehovah Nissi
The Lord My Banner

Jehovah Raah
The Lord My Shepherd

Jehovah Rapha
The Lord That Heals

Jehovah Shammah
The Lord Is There

Jehovah Tsidkenu
The Lord Our Righteousness

Jehovah Mekoddishkem
The Lord Who Sanctifies You

El Olam
The Everlasting God

Elohim
God

Jehovah Jireh
The Lord Will Provide

Jehovah Shalom
The Lord Is Peace

Jehovah Sabaoth
The Lord of Hosts

~A Survivors Prayer~

Heavenly Father,

Most gracious and All-knowing God. I come to you as a humble servant of the gospel of truth. Lord, I surrender all pride, arrogance, haughtiness, bitterness, shame and resentment. I come thanking you for my trials and tribulations. Father, I see you ever so clearly, as my soul beckons you. I thank you Lord, for saving me, my children and generations to come. I thank you because you have given me victory in all things and in all truth pertaining to all matters of the heart. Your destiny for my life, breathes and takes root. I thank you for the spirit of truth and boldness. Thank you, Lord for your word that is a lamp unto my feet and a light unto my path. Thank you for supplying all my needs and granting me with renewed strength daily. Thank you for the valleys and mountaintops of my life. Thank you, Heavenly Father, that all things work together for my good.

Lord, I need you to help me in every area of my life. Nothing gets passed your omniscience. Grant me a keen sense of discernment. Bless me with a heightened level of awareness that propels me to stand on my feet. It will drive me to take the steps I need to take. Help me to see the resources, the programs, the legal help and community that are available to me. God, I thank you for going before me, dispatching your ministering and warring angels.

I bind the enemy of fear, false tactics, lies, deceit and intimidation. I bind anxiety, worry, defeat, depression and oppression. I declare that the enemy shall be ensnared in his/her own ways. The *false* truth will not prevail. I declare that you will be my mouthpiece as you were the mouthpiece for Moses before Pharaoh. I thank you that every chain collapse and every tormenting spirit would flee. I thank you that the time is now and that there are no untimely delays. I thank you for spiritual intelligence, spiritual knowledge and that the laws of heaven set out, shall be completed. You did not give me the spirit of fear, but of love, power and a sound mind. Decrease me and increase your Holy Spirit. Lord through all of this, my voice, my stance, my posture is in you and from you. Give me the keys to unlock the truth and the everlasting power to dismantle the enemy and be set free.

Shut down the enemy and it's deceitful/blind witnesses. Give me the spiritual articulation to bring about an awareness. Let that awareness expose eye-opening facts that foils the enemies plans of destruction. Let it reach those who have been exposed or directly abused by the enemy of lies and torment. They have been trespassed against at home, at work and through the judicial system and law enforcement. Cover and bless all the people, agencies, angels who have prayed, sacrificed and labored on behalf of my family, my children and me. Open your heavenly portal, now God and unlock the doors to victory, destiny and purpose. Let my purpose be stirred in such a way that I do not cower or bow down to the enemy of distraction or intimidation. Help me to keep my eyes on the cross and the truth that will set captives free.

Set out your plan, your strategy. Reveal to my counsel/advocate(s) and me every step of the way what to do, what to say and what to bring to the light of truth. Help me to be bold and courageous where I need to be bold and courageous. Let the schemes and tactics of the opposing party be dismantled on their false post and the bomb of Gilead crumble them to the ground. Let not my will be done, but your will be done. Let the enemy's plan be undone and destroyed. Let my mourning turn to joy and give me beauty for my ashes.

Now Father, I pray to put on the full armor of you. The helmet of righteousness, the sandals of peace, the sword of your word, the shield of faith and the belt of truth. God grant me the serenity to accept the things that I cannot change, the strength to change the things that I can and the wisdom to know the difference. It is in your precious, holy, magnificent name that I pray and ask all these things to be done.

Amen!

- *This prayer can be tailored by the reader to meet specific prayer request and needs.*

Directory of Help
National Resources & Helpful Links

Victims of Crime Resource Center
(800) 842-8467

National Center for Victims of Crime
(855) 4VICTIM
(855) 484-2846

24-hour hotline and link to local resources
www.victimconnect.org

National Domestic Violence Hotline
(800) 799-SAFE
(800)799-7233
(800) 787-3224 (TDD)
www.thehotline.org

National Hope Line Network
(800) SUICIDE
(800) 784-2433
www.hopeline.com

Love is Respect (National Dating Abuse Calling Line)
(866) 331-9474
www.loveisrespect.org

Suicide Prevention Line
(877) 727-4747

Peer to Peer Crisis Teen Line
(800) 852-8336
www.teenlineonline.org

Suicide Hotline
(800) 784-2433
www.suicide.org

Suicide Hotline for Teens
(866) 210-3388
www.thursdayschild.org

Victim Information and Notification Everyday (VINE)
(877) 411-5588 (Status of inmate changes)

2-1-1/Info link
(Local State Directory) 211

National Victim Center
(800) FYI-CALL

Suggested Reading

The Gift of Fear
Gavin D. Becker

Coping with Trauma
Jon Allen

Crime Victims' Guide to Justice
Mary L Boland

Embracing the Fear
Judith Bemis

The Four Agreements
Don Miguel Ruiz

Gifts from a Course in Miracles
Frances Vaughan & Roger Walsh

The Grieving Teen-
A Guide for Teenagers & Their Friends
Helen Fitzgerald

Life After Trauma
Dena Rosenbloom & Mary Beth
Williams with Barbara Watkins

The Power of Now
Eckhart Jolle

The PTSD Workbook
Mary Beth Williams

Stop Domestic Violence
Lou Brown

What to do When the Police Leave
Bill Jenkins

About the Author

Maury Danielle, a native of Long Beach California is a divorced mother of two beautiful children. She has devoted her life to ensuring not only her children are healthy and whole, but families all over the world. Maury Danielle is a natural encourager and was drawn to environments that were conducive to ministering to those in need. She has a "gift of faith" and has always believed God for the impossible. However, Maury's faith would be tested beyond what she could ever imagine over a ten-year span of time. She experienced physical, emotional, psychological, verbal and sexual abuse, which changed the trajectory of the life she envisioned. Consequently, she lost everything that she knew in friendships, family, marriage, money, lifestyle and reputation. She literally hit rock bottom, spiraling into depression and coming to terms with the false narratives that she had lived by for years.

Maury was determined to be well and experience true wholeness, so she had to do something different in order to achieve something different. She battled with and identified internal and external challenges that would serve as a catalyst to identifying the root of her personal struggles. This led to a spiritual journey that forced her to travel through the birth canal of destiny and experience a rebirth. As a result, God has blessed her with a new birth in Him. Maury made the choice to do the work of setting herself free and freeing her children from generational despondency. She looked deep within herself to uncover the lies that she believed about herself and replaced them with the truth of who God says she is… and who He has called her to be. Maury has truly become a life champion through life challenges.

Maury became an entrepreneur by the time she was 12-years old. She is a spirit-filled, passionate, astute businesswoman and author. Although Maury was born in California, she was raised in the Midwest. Later she moved to Texas where she grew not only in her business acumen, but also as a spiritual leader. Her spiritual journey deepened when she transitioned back to California.

Maury is gifted in many areas. This book is the first of many powerful, wisdom-filled, and anointed books that will come through this talented author.

Made in the
USA
Lexington, KY